Managing in the New Economy

*Performance Management Habits
to renew organizations for the new millennium*

André de Waal

Morel Fourman

Foreword by
Jeff Papows
President and CEO, Lotus Development Corporation

ARTHUR
ANDERSEN

büsiness
GROUPWARE BUSINESS INTELLIGENCE

To Hank, with warm best wishes and Thaks,

Morel Fourman

Oct 08

Published in the United Kingdom in 2000 by:

Arthur Andersen
Oostmaaslaan 71
Rotterdam 3006 AM
The Netherlands

and

Show Business Software Limited
137 Euston Road
London NW1 2AA
England

Cover design by the Parkway Partnership.
Illustrations by Arthur Andersen (Netherlands) and Show
Business Software Ltd.

ISBN 0 9537 820 0 X, Show Business Software Ltd.

Printed and bound in Great Britain by the Parkway
Partnership.

CONTENTS

Acknowledgements

The authors would like to thank the following people for contributing to shaping this book, either in technical development, content or for the logistics. First thanks to our customers and clients for being our patient best teachers.

Thanks to Sarah Foyle for her commitment and detailed editing and to Rachel Riley for breathing life into the case study and for helping to make it all make sense. Thanks to the core development team from Show Business, Arthur Andersen and Lotus who have implemented the ideas described in this book in the Action Driven Balanced Scorecard. Thanks to David Reid, who has translated business requirements into an elegant technical solution with the partnership, commitment and efforts of: Eric van Engen, Madelon Kleynen, Chris Reynolds and Patrick Söhlke.

Thanks also to: Howard Almond, Felicienne Bloemers, Jim Dinsmore, Hans Fermont, Mick Fernhout, Sacha van Geene, Julie Jones, Saskia Kuneman, Jiske Kuyper, John Masters, Kobien Mijland, Adrian Reason, Sriyani Tanner, Albert Werkman, Jon Wheeler, Anand Doshi, Swapnil Paranjpe, Rajeev Kumar, Uma Joshi, Srikanth Adiga and Shridhar Shukla.

Thanks go to the following people who gave detailed input on Creating Internal Partnership and who are all practitioners in this area. Rob Kendall for his work on buy-in and his partnership with Show Business. Mike Griffiths for his breakthrough coaching of the Show Business team and for his help in clarifying the relationship between vision, implementation and breakthrough performance. Mark Fourman for insightful feedback and sharing the benefits of his experience. Thanks to Birgitta Schomaker and John Shuttleworth for their excellent comments on the various versions of the chapter on Creating Internal Partnership. Thanks to John Case for the contribution he has made to organizational effectiveness, by researching and writing on the subject of Open Book Management.

And finally, we would like to thank our partners Linda and Gina for their love and support in this project.

Foreword

by
Jeff Papows
President and CEO, Lotus Development Corporation

'**Managing in the New Economy**' is an especially timely book on organizational effectiveness in light of the dramatic technological forces that have been unleashed by the Internet and that are changing the very landscape of how we conduct global business. Based on Arthur Andersen's best-practice study, spanning business processes, collaborative technologies, and the vital dynamic of organizational culture, 'Managing in the New Economy' sets out a compelling agenda for renewing our organizations in the new millennium.

The authors shine a spotlight on the all important questions in front of every large enterprise: What is next after the massive technology investments made to prepare for Y2K? How can organizations turn their investments in ERP (Enterprise Resource Planning) software into measurable business returns? This book is of primary value due to the answers it provides to these pressing questions. Furthermore, it demonstrates that to deliver required returns, we must begin with the creation of organizational cultures and practices that harness the power and passion of people first. It demonstrates clearly that the way people in an organization relate to one another - 'the personality or even soul of an organization' is essential to achieving organizational effectiveness. For many of us at Lotus, the last ten years have been a labor of love driven by our passion for helping people within large organizations to collaborate effectively and hone their competitive edges to achieve increasingly higher business returns. As we discovered through the research into social sciences conducted by the Lotus Institute, collaboration begins and ends with people, not with technology alone. It is therefore gratifying to see our basic philosophical foundation validated within the pages of 'Managing in the New Economy'.

The authors demonstrate that performance management - setting a vision, a strategy, tracking results, taking corrective actions when needed and learning from mistakes - is key to Organizational Effectiveness.

As a veteran product strategist for Lotus' communications offerings, I live and breathe what technology can do to help organizations. And as a CEO, I know that steering an organization takes a lot more than just technology. I am reminded of an analogy used by Buckminster Fuller to describe how to achieve large scale change: if you want to change the direction of a large oil tanker, you can't do it by just pushing on the bow of the tanker. It's too heavy. The next step is to try to push the rudder at the back of the tanker. Even the rudder is too big and heavy. At the back of a rudder, is another much smaller rudder, called the trim tab. To steer the ship, you adjust the trim tab, the trim tab steers the rudder into a new position and the rudder steers the tanker.

Performance management is the trim tab for steering organizations. Every CEO and every manager needs to be able to steer effectively. This book provides invaluable insight into how we can use the team we have in place today to steer an organization - to strategically effect course corrections at crucial moments - in today's business environment using existing technologies.

Above all, the authors provide irrefutable 'bottom-line' rationales as to why we must create organizations that are derived from the spirits and hearts of their people, and inspire the commitment of those same people that is so essential to success in our global economy.

Jeff Papows
Cambridge, Mass.
January 2000

Section 1: Introduction

1. PERFORMANCE MANAGEMENT: THE KEY TO THRIVING IN THE NEW ECONOMY

KEY POINTS

☑ The New Economy requires new levels of speed, flexibility and Organizational Effectiveness.

☑ Performance management is key to Organizational Effectiveness.

☑ Organizations that manage by measures are more successful.

☑ Effective performance management requires a combination of the right business model, the right technology and a paradigm, or working culture, of partnership.

Are you ready for the New Economy?

The last few years of the twentieth century have seen a rapid increase in the speed of virtually all business processes. Speed of innovation has become increasingly important, while the competitive advantage from innovation lasts less and less time. The 24-hour economy makes it possible to continuously do business and interact with customers and partners. The explosion of the Internet and corporate intranets and the rush to implement ERP (Enterprise Resource Planning) software has transformed the nature of business processes. Managing and using knowledge has become a vital competitive tool. The value of an organization is no longer determined only in terms of tangible assets but also in intangible assets and in the quality of its workforce. Competing for the resource of human talent is vital to the success of every organization. So, in order to thrive, organizations need to be great places to work. Even with the right people, organizations cannot afford to be complacent because there is always a would-be competitor waiting. These changes in the business environment, the massive shift of capital into

.COM businesses and the investment in e-business by businesses and governments, guarantee that the way we do business in the new millennium will be very different from the way we have done business in the past. This *New Economy* brings with it immense opportunities and new challenges.

Born-on-the-web, .COM businesses are exploding into existence – leaping from start-up to global prominence. Their implementation and performance management challenges are different from the challenges of established organizations, which are developing the agility to survive and prosper in the New Economy. Our focus in this book is on managing business which have evolved in the 'old' economy to prepare for the speed and flexibility required in the New Economy.

Embracing the New Economy requires organizations to change the way they work. Effective performance management is a vital ingredient for change. If change does not happen fast enough, even though the will is present, the organization will fail. The organizations that prosper from the New Economy and the e-business revolution will not be those with the best plans, but those with the best implementation and change skills. Transforming business processes is changing the role of people from 'doers' (who operate as steps/stages within processes) into 'implementers' (who must execute programs to create, monitor, understand and improve processes). The more we transform and automate business processes, the more we need to measure and manage in order to maintain quality and improve performance. Therefore, the performance management process has an important role to play in helping organizations to make the transition into the New Economy.

Performance management allows an organization to think intelligently and act effectively. It closes the feedback loop between the data in business processes and the people who take action to make things happen. It helps people to apply their individual intelligence to making good decisions and it helps them to manage the actions that create value for the organization.

If managing an organization is compared to driving a vehicle, the implementation Habits of high-performing organizations described in this book provide the clear windscreen, the speedometer, the steering wheel and brake needed to effectively guide, direct and control. Performance management is an essential tool for the top team of an organization in implementing strategy, but it is also an essential discipline for every manager who wants to succeed in the New Economy.

☐ Perceived as an industry leader over the past 3 years

▣ Reported to be financially ranked in the Top 3 of their industry

▣ Last major cultural or operational change judged to be very or moderately successful

Source: American Management Association, Survey by The William Schiemann & Associates

Figure 1.1: Performance-managed companies are more successful

Research shows time and again the importance of the performance management process to the success of an organization, whether this success is measured financially or not. This was the case in the *old* economy, and performance management is even more important in the fast lane of the *New Economy*.

This book begins to answer questions like:

• What does world class performance management look like?

• How can we implement best practice?

• How can we use technology to support best practice?

The book also provides information to help you to answer questions about your own organization's performance management process:

- Is there sufficient action tracking? Can we use performance management to make sure that our next change program is a success?
- Can our organization be better prepared to satisfy the need for speed?
- How can we meet and exceed the benchmark targets set by our competitors?

And finally . . .

Is our performance management ready for the New Economy?

This book provides a first glimpse of how best practice performance management can help to prepare a business for the New Economy. It combines vision and practicality by providing an understanding of why new levels of performance management are needed, looking at what is possible and understanding how it can be achieved. The book is based on the 1999 global best practice benchmark study on performance management performed by Arthur Andersen Business Consulting. It incorporates critical success factors identified from IBM e-business and communications infrastructure projects with insights from leading transformational and change consultants and experience gained during executive coaching and change programs. Our goal is to help you and your organization to thrive in the New Economy.

Why top managers need good performance management

We all work *hard* enough and *long* enough already. Working *smarter* comes from doing the right things and doing them effectively. In a changing business environment, performance management is essential if 'knowledge workers' are to continue to make good decisions and work effectively in the new environment. In high-performing organizations, everyone needs tools to continually adjust (in alignment with the strategy and goals of the organization) and to support their performance. Strategy setting and delivery must be owned by everybody in the organization. It is top management's task to steer and coach the organization to maintain alignment and to deliver a strategy. The top team also has to make sure that there is co-ordination across organizational departments. The top team's challenge is not so much to 'develop a strategy' as to create an organization that knows its strategy and is able to deliver it.

High Performing Organizations

'Flaky' = High Vision Poor Implementation	High Performance = High Vision Good Implementation
Going Nowhere = Low Vision Poor Implementation	Conservative = Low Vision Good Implementation

Vision

Performance Management =
Plan + Measure + Corrective Action

Figure 1.2: The characteristics of high-performing organizations

High-performing organizations have both vision and the ability to implement. With vision and no ability to implement, the organization is ineffective and 'flaky'. With implementation ability and no vision, the organization is conservative but, again, ineffective. These companies tend to be followers, so they miss out on market opportunity. With both vision and implementation ability, the organization has the essentials of high performance. To move an organization from a low- to a high-performer ultimately requires a shift of attention from monitoring results to taking action, from running processes to creating predictable and sustained value by creating, transforming and managing processes. To locate your own organization on this grid, think of what happened with your last change initiative and of the last time you introduced a new product, service or technology successfully.

Our experience shows that the power of an organization to become high performing can be dramatically increased by managing three key areas within a common vision:

- change management, or more powerfully, **Paradigm management**, as facilitated by ...

- the **performance management process** and enabled by a ...

- **groupware** and **communications infrastructure**.

1. Paradigm Management

Paradigm Management has the same objective as Change Management but it focuses on the root causes of resistance to change, not just symptoms. One person's support and another person's resistance to change come from a difference in point-of-view or 'Paradigm'. Managing Paradigm helps to dam-bust blocks to change and helps to create a culture of internal partnership focused on delivering the strategy.

2. Performance Management Process

The best practice performance management process described here uses Key Value Drivers and the Balanced Scorecard as the focus for implementation through accountability. It supports continual improvement through systematic capture and sharing of learnings. The process manages corrective, preventative and breakthrough actions to deliver the business results that implement the strategy and goals. Action is the most important part of any performance management process, yet many organizations only measure performance without systematically defining and managing actions that impact those measures.

3. Groupware and Communications Infrastructure

Delivering best-practice performance management requires three levels of electronic communications support:

- **Communication** – email;

- **Collaboration** – co-creation and sharing of knowledge; and

- **Co-ordination** - collaborating in time and process

Often the choice of groupware and communications infrastructure is delegated to technical committees, which make no reference to the needs of the performance management process. As a result, some organizations use a communications infrastructure which only supports email, thereby crippling the organization in its ability to co-create and share knowledge, collaborate in the vital performance management process, and to manage action.

Many organizations sabotage their chances of delivering on strategy and goals by dealing with these issues in different functional silos from which it is hard to see the 'big picture' of what the organization needs. The issues are owned by different parts of the organization, perhaps using different, uncoordinated, or even competing partners or suppliers, so the whole organization is ineffective. Co-ordinated leadership effort and sponsorship in these areas by the top team can deliver massive return across the organization.

This book identifies Habits that support best practice performance management and Paradigm management. It also outlines a technology solution that supports those Habits, at the level of departmental initiatives and overall strategy. The aim of this book is to provide simple insights that are easy to implement and which make a difference to the effectiveness of people and organizations.

2. THE CALL FOR ACTION!

KEY POINTS

☑ To succeed in the New Economy requires excellence in implementation.

☑ High-performing organizations are able to create a vision and implement it.

☑ Performance management is key to successful implementation.

☑ Only 10% of organizations deliver on their strategy.

☑ 90% of organizations identify that a clear, action-oriented understanding of the strategy would significantly influence their strategic and operational success.

☑ The main cause of CEOs failing is the inability to implement the strategic vision.

☑ An action-oriented approach to performance management is required, rather than just passive measuring of performance.

☑ Based on a 50-company global benchmark study, implementation Habits that enable high performance have been identified.

☑ Intranets and groupware technology make it possible to support these Habits across an enterprise, department or team.

The need for change: from measurement to action management

"The purpose of information is not knowledge. It is being able to take the right action."

Peter F. Drucker
Management Challenges for the 21st Century

Managers and companies are increasingly under pressure to create new initiatives, develop plans and deliver on the results they promise. Challenges must be transformed into solutions that work - in weeks instead of years. Effective performance management enables an organization to develop quality strategic plans, set ambitious targets and track performance to ensure that objectives are delivered. A new action-oriented, closed-loop approach to performance management, supported by technology is enabling new levels of reliability in implementation. Just as every organization needs its accounting or Enterprise Resource Planning (ERP) systems to *do* operational business, each also needs its performance management system to *manage and improve* the achievement of strategic objectives and goals.

In the last few years, attention has been focusing on articulating strategy and measuring performance. Balanced Scorecards, value-based management, critical success factors, key performance indicators and activity-based management are enhancing the ability of companies to measure the state of their businesses. However, measuring is not enough. To be effective, managers and organizations must shift attention from *measurement* to *action management*.

Recent research (Renaissance, 1996; De Waal e.a., 1997; Redwood e.a., 1999; Charan e.a., 1999; Drucker, 1999) indicates that organizations have difficulty in turning their strategic intent into activities that achieve strategic goals. Time after time, although organizations often have a good strategic plan in place, they are not able to communicate and implement this plan effectively. They are therefore not able to deliver on their strategic goals. The main challenge for CEOs today is not to have a good strategy but to implement the strategy. For an organization to thrive, managers must be able to get things done, to deliver on commitments, to follow up on critical assignments and to support and to hold people accountable for their promises.

90% of organizations polled confirmed that clear, action-oriented deployment of their strategy would significantly influence their success in dealing with this pressure. Their managers need to replace passive reporting **performance measurement** with pro-active, results-oriented **performance management**. What does it take to create breakthrough performance? The right vision is essential, but what about implementation? How do some organizations manage to envision new territory and boldly go there, while others give up on their visions because they seem to be inevitably stuck? High-performing organizations are recognizing that their performance management process, with its accompanying flow of information and knowledge, is critical to their success. These organizations realize that some of the most important knowledge in their organization is the performance management knowledge that drives the business. With a high-quality performance management process, they have a clear understanding of their internal and external environments and the ability to respond quickly and effectively. These organizations can adapt quickly to changing circumstances and are positioned well to take advantage of possibilities and inevitable rapid chances in the New Economy.

High-performing organizations see their performance management process as the process that enables them to deliver a predictable contribution to sustained value-creation, even in the face of a changing environment. This performance management process has five parts:

1. *Strategy Development* – Creating strategic action plans for measurable performance improvement, based on a thorough understanding of the key value drivers and aimed at achieving a competitive advantage.

2. *Target setting* – Creating clear operational action plans for improving the key value drivers (measures), for committing resources, and for setting financial targets for the coming period.

3. *Performance Measurement* – Collecting, processing (including consolidating) and distributing data and information, to allow effective strategy development and target setting.

4. *Performance Review* – Reviewing actual performance, targets and forecasts, to make sure that preventative and corrective actions are taken to keep the company on track.

5. *Incentive Compensation* – Linking the effects of strategic and operational actions on key value drivers with compensation and benefits.

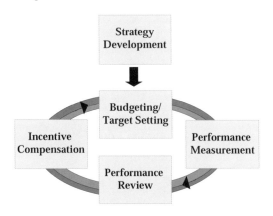

Figure 2.1: The parts in the Performance Management process

To achieve high-performance, organizations must have the ability to implement strategy. Excellence in performance management is key to effective implementation. To improve and excel in performance management, we need to answer the following questions:

- How are we doing performance management today?
- What can we learn from best practice organizations?
- How can we adapt and implement best practice?

How are we doing performance management today: the MIRA

The first question - 'How are we doing performance management today?' - can be answered by applying the Management Information and Reporting Analysis (MIRA) in your organization. In the MIRA, the quality of an organization's management information and reporting is evaluated on the basis of eight dimensions. The choice of dimensions is based on our project experience and is consistent with findings from comprehensive studies of relevant literature. The management reporting system can be measured on the following dimensions:

- *Internal financial*   Insight into financial affairs to the right level, with the right content.

- *Non-financial*   Non-financial data linked to strategy via critical success factors and key performance indicators.

- *Dynamics*   Management information is used in analysis of results, decision-making, action-taking, monitoring of results, and evaluation of the actions taken.

- *Communication*   People regularly share information about the results in a structured manner across horizontal and vertical organizational boundaries.

- *Systems support*   Information systems provide a stable structure for quick collection, processing, reporting and sharing of financial and non-financial information and related knowledge and actions.

- *User-friendliness*   Reports are easy to use and understand and have the right level of detail.

- *Integrity*   Information provided is timely, reliable, consistent and complete.

- *Target-setting*   Continuous improvement is achieved by setting and measuring against targets for critical processes, including benchmarking against other organizations.

The results of a MIRA are depicted in a Radar Diagram, which identifies the areas in which an organization is week compared to best practice: these are indicated in the diagram by the valleys between the peaks. In the radar diagram below, it is clear that the organization is weak in use of non-financial indicators and in ease of use of their management reporting.

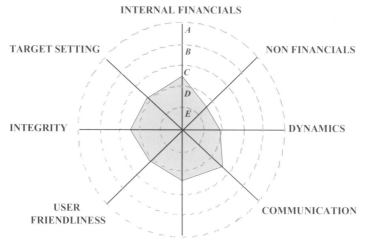

Figure 2.2: Example of a MIRA Radar Diagram

Appendix B also lists some of the key learning points/recommendations from over 50 MIRAs carried out around the world. To perform your own MIRA, visit www.showbusiness.com.

What can we learn from best practice organizations: the Habits

Recently, we undertook a global benchmark study of high-performing organizations (Arthur Andersen Business Consulting, 1999). This benchmark study focused on the performance management systems (processes and information technology) which enable high-performing companies to fulfill on their vision and strategy. The goal of the study was to identify re-usable best practice relating to the performance management process.

The benchmark study took us across industry sectors, cultures and management styles. During the analysis of the study, and by combining this analysis with the results of the 50 MIRAs, we began to see that these high-performing companies had certain common performance management 'Habits' that were clear and, even, simple. We did not *invent* these Habits, we *recognized* them - just as Newton did not invent gravity but was the first to put a label on it. Each Habit provides opportunities for organizations to improve their performance management process. *Overall, the Habits allow an organization to deliver on desired outcomes, by continually learning and improving.*

The implementation Habits we identified are described below.

Habit 1: Deliver on the strategy and goals

Understand what is strategically important to the organization and make sure it is measured and monitored. Translate strategy into critical success factors and key performance indicators. Track progress over time. Combine financial with non-financial, lagging with leading and cause with effect indicators in a Balanced Scorecard, to provide a strategic and balanced view for decision-making.

Habit 2: Create and manage internal partnership

Create an organization in which people can win together. Make sure that the people in the organization know what they need to do and that they have 'bought-in' to achieving the strategy. Change the management style and culture to make it possible to use all of the Habits effectively.

Habit 3: Keep it simple

Focus on a small number of value drivers: measures that drive performance. Align activities with improving these value drivers.

Habit 4: Manage by exception

Report on exceptions, to focus attention where it is needed.

Habit 5: Manage by action

Identify corrective actions designed to overcome existing problems, and design preventative actions to resolve forecasted problems before they actually happen. To profit from the opportunities and overcome the challenges of the New Economy, create breakthrough actions to produce results beyond predictions and 'outside the box'. Target the impact of actions and track them from inception to completion, systematically capturing and sharing learning.

Habit 6: Create information transparency

Remove the labor from information gathering, delivery and presentation. Provide a one-stop-shop for everyone to access performance management knowledge, but only that to which they are entitled.

Habit 7: Leverage technology

Use technology including Intranet and groupware, to embed and support good practice and link into the systems which run the business to support the systems which help to manage the business.

The process, technology AND people-related Habits work together to enable effective implementation, learning and high performance.

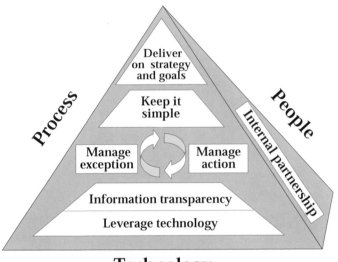

Technology

Figure 2.3: The implementation habits of high-performing organizations

The diagram above shows how delivering on the **strategy** is achieved by keeping the performance management process **simple** – with Key Value Drivers. **Exception** reporting is used to make sure that problems and opportunities are seen quickly so that **action** can be taken immediately. To make this work across an organization and to allow for cross-organizational learning, there must be **information transparency,** which is achieved by **leveraging technology.** All of the Habits rely on **internal partnership.**

The following table outlines some of the key findings of our benchmark study and of the 50 MIRAs, together with the performance management Habit(s) to which each relates.

Process & findings	Habit
Strategy development process	
To achieve breakthrough results, strategic plans must start from a purpose and vision of the future, not the constraints of the past.	Habit 2: Create and manage internal partnership
To invoke people's commitment, the vision of the future must be a 'game worth playing', both in terms of personal reward and the vision to be achieved for the organization.	Habit 2: Create and manage internal partnership
Strategic plans must be based on a balanced set of leading and lagging value drivers.	Habit 1: Deliver the strategy and goals
Strategic plans must be outward looking so that external influences are taken into account when formulating long-term views. This avoids consolidation of plans to give unrealistic rapid growth projections for future performance.	Habit 1: Deliver the strategy and goals
Strategic plans must be based around creating value for customers through taking action.	Habit 1: Deliver the strategy and goals Habit 5: Manage by action
Budgeting	
Focus the budget on a few key value drivers to avoid wasted time on details that will not effect performance.	Habit 3: Keep it simple
Use technology to support finalizing the budget to save time-consuming effort in manual iteration.	Habit 6: Information transparency Habit 7: Leverage technology
Budget for improvements in the core business, as well as for implementing the strategic plan.	Habit 1: Deliver the strategy and goals
Simplify: don't spend the whole year on next year's budget. (Remember Parkinson's Law: work expands to fit the time available.)	Habit 3: Keep it simple

Process & findings	Habit
Performance Measurement	
Improve formal steering and control tools	Habit 2: Create and manage internal partnership
Manage by exception	Habit 1: Deliver the strategy and goals
Include non-financial information in reports	Habit 1: Deliver the strategy and goals
Implement performance action management	Habit 5: Manage by action
Formulate the role of management in steering on results	Habit 2: Create and manage internal partnership Habit 4: Manage by exception Habit 5: Manage by action
Integrate the performance management process	Habit 3: Keep it simple
Performance Review	
Forecasts must be reasonably accurate to add value in the performance review process.	Habit 1: Deliver the strategy and goals
Keep forecasts simple, without too much detail to avoid wasted effort.	Habit 3: Keep it simple
Use technology to support forecasting to save time and effort.	Habit 7: Leverage technology
Make performance review meetings exception-based.	Habit 4: Manage by exception
Incentive Compensation [1]	
Base incentive pay on more than financial targets.	Habit 1: Deliver the strategy and goals
Do not try to buy commitment, build a Paradigm of internal partnership and acknowledge contribution through financial reward.	Habit 2: Create and manage internal partnership

---

- [1] Because the benchmark study was not focused on the incentive compensation, only limited attention is paid to this sub-process.

Managers at all levels are stressed with ambitious targets but often receive inadequate information and knowledge for effective management. Managers need the tools to shift attention from measuring performance to managing performance. Organizations need to achieve this shift enterprise-wide. The Habits are applicable to an individual, team or departmental manager, as much as to a large corporation. For any manager with a target, these Habits provide a simple checklist to support effectiveness and reduce stress.

A CEO, an organization or an individual manager, can use the implementation Habits to help get everyone aligned and doing the right thing and doing it right. That is what it is all about: to work smarter and to deliver results, in spite of the circumstances, the competition, and the challenging issues facing the organization.

How can we implement best practice: a Performance Management Portal

Our research shows that organizations need flexible systems support for implementation of their vision and strategy, especially when individuals responsible are distributed across locations, countries and time zones.

We have distilled the key business requirements from our work with champions of performance management projects to describe a performance management portal that fulfills these needs. Our goal in writing this book is to enable you to support high-performing teams and organizations based on this experience. Today, some of the world's leading organizations are using a performance management portal which we have developed in partnership with them. Our goal in developing it was to support cross-organizational learning in performance management. The ideas behind this book have taken on a life of their own – developing from the shared insight and experience of implementation champions, practitioners and consultants.

To be applicable in today's fast-changing organizations, a performance management portal has to be configured fast and has to be flexible enough to evolve and change with the business it is helping to manage. And because people are now more empowered and responsibility is pushed down the organization, today's performance management system has to have the ability to scale, to cascade down the entire organization and across business units.

Until recently, this combination of requirements could not be met without extensive customization, resulting in unacceptable risk, cost and implementation lead times. The groupware infrastructure and intranets of today's organizations have changed the situation completely, creating a turning point in what is possible in performance management and, therefore, in organizational performance. High-performing organizations are building their management knowledge into technology solutions that help them to deliver on strategy. Instead of practicing performance management in the boardroom and executive office, they are enabling pervasive management of performance. A performance management portal can deliver huge business value when it can be cascaded down the organization, delivering accountability where it is needed (on the frontline). The Habits help managers to shift from measuring performance to managing performance, from being the soccer ball to being the player scoring goals for the organization. The turning point for organizations happens as these Habits are applied pervasively, which is made possible by intranet and groupware infrastructure. In Chapter 10, we describe an example to show what is possible.

Case Study: Introducing UltraViolet Design Ltd.

Each of the following seven chapters of this book describes one of the high-performance Habits, identifying key points and highlighting the related issues and challenges which managers and organizations are facing. The way in which ADBS supports the Habits is illustrated using a case study. In this case study an organization called UltraViolet Design Ltd. is followed on its journey to become a high-performing organization by implementing a high quality, performance management process. The company is further introduced below. You may want to skip from chapter to chapter in order to get an overview of the Habits before reading the case study.

Alternatively, you can read the case study as you read about each Habit and see how the Habits are put into practice. The case study is relevant to large corporations because it suggests how an agile competitor may be preparing to take your market. The case study is relevant to small businesses because it shows that any business can use e-business to break into new markets and expand. The case study company is not big (size doesn't matter) - or located at the centre of its target market (location doesn't matter), but its management team has enough pain and/or ambition to prompt it into action.

In 1987, the Williams brothers established the company UltraViolet Design Ltd (UVD). The company started with some promising designs of high quality home products, including vases, lamps and clocks. The General Manager of the company is John Williams, who is also responsible for the design of the products. His brother, Gary, has responsibility for the manufacturing of the products and their brother, Martin, is in charge of Marketing & Sales.

The brothers strongly emphasize innovation, ecological soundness, quality and market/customer orientation. This emphasis has produced results. Over the past twelve years, the turnover has increased on average 15% per year. The number of employees has grown from an initial 6 to 256. UVD has now penetrated the top tier of the retail market segment: the top furniture stores, department stores and specialist stores.

Initially, the brothers only aimed at the Dutch market. However, Martin, who likes travelling in Europe during his weekends and holidays, noticed that there was a market for UVD products throughout Europe. He had a particularly good feeling about the UK. He developed a catalog containing UVD's products and mailed this catalog to retailers all over Europe. His marketing instinct was correct; European sales increased, especially in England.

Four years ago, when the European sales surpassed the marketing and sales capacity of the Dutch office, a new office was opened in the UK. At that time, almost 35% of UVD's sales were in the UK. Marketing, sales and warehousing activities for the UK are sourced from the UK office (UVD UK). Because Martin likes travelling, and since he was already responsible for Marketing & Sales, he was appointed as CEO of the UK operation.

The Headquarters of UVD Europe, still based in the Netherlands, is responsible for:

- Marketing & Sales (excluding the USA & UK)
- Customer Service
- Manufacturing of the products.
- Research & Development of the products
- Finance
- Personnel

Recently, the brothers decided to penetrate the North-American market with their designer products. Setting up a complete distribution network all over the North American continent was far beyond the financial capacity of UVD. They decided to market and sell their products over the Internet. John hired a new manager, Jack Coopers, who set up the UVD Web site and out-sourced the warehousing and logistics handling of the products to a national distributor. The brothers are now working enthusiastically to make Internet sales take off.

After over 15 years of working together, the brothers and their employees are used to working as a close team. However, there is a marked decrease in enthusiasm compared to the eagerness and excitement everyone experienced when the business was being established. The UK and North American operations benefit from being new divisions, able to create themselves newly. However, employees in The Netherlands, in particular, find the companies growth difficult and stressful as they adapt to include new procedures and processes.

UltraViolet Design's organizational structure looks like this:

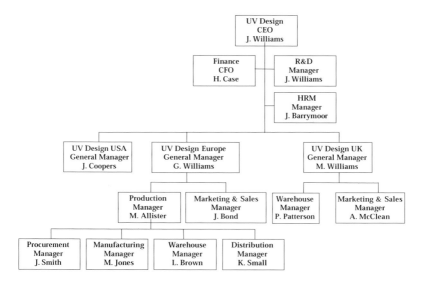

Figure 2.4: UltraViolet Design's organizational chart

UltraViolet Design produces and sells four types of product, namely Vases, Lamps, Clocks and CD-racks. Each product group contains a range of products - these are shown in the following table:

Product group	Product type	Product Name
Vase	Large Vase	Dali
	Medium Vase	Brood
	Small Vase	Esscher
Lamp	Hanging lamp	Picasso
	Standing lamp	Monet
	Wall lamp	Gaugin

Product group	Product type	Product Name
Clock	Wall clock	Mondriaan
		Rembrandt
	Standing clock	Appel
		Goch
CD-rack	30 CD's	Mozart
	40 CD's	Bach
	50 CD's	Chopin

John Williams is most proud of his master creation: the Clock product group. All clocks, except the Appel, are made of lightweight, re-cycleable, synthetic material and have an ingenious clock mechanism that automatically adjusts to the relevant local world time. This means that in the UK, for example, the clock automatically adjusts to Greenwich Mean Time (GMT) and in The Netherlands to Central European Time (CET). John's latest creation is an ecologically sound CD-rack. It has a revolutionary click mechanism to facilitate the task of sliding the CDs in and out of the rack. Because of this click mechanism, the CDs can be stored very close together, reducing the size of the rack. The product (in all three sizes) was put into production at the end of 1998 and was brought to market in May of 1999.

Together John and Gary redesigned the Monet lamp and the Appel clock and changed the raw material to make them ecologically sound as well. They had initially committed to customers to deliver the products in January of 1999 but, due to production problems, this was postponed to February and April respectively for each product.

The table shown below gives an overview of the distribution channels for sales by country.

Area	Country	Regions	Distribution channel
Europe (UVD Netherlands)	The Netherlands	North South West East Central	Furniture stores Department stores Specialist stores
	Belgium	Central	Furniture stores Department stores
	Luxembourg	Central	Furniture stores
	Germany	West	Furniture stores Department stores
	France	North	Furniture stores
	Spain	North	Furniture stores Department stores
	Italy	Central	Furniture stores
UK (UVD UK)	UK	North South West East Central	Furniture stores Department stores Specialist stores
Americas (UVD USA)	Americas	North America South America (with focus on the north)	Internet (warehousing and distribution are out-sourced)

In the first years, the UK office mainly focused on the furniture stores and the department stores. Now the focus is being expanded to specialist stores.

In 1999, customers were disgruntled by the delay in the delivery of the new Appel clock and Monet lamp as stock was received too late to incorporate into the spring catalogs. Sales were affected by this ommission and Manufacturing hurried to fill late orders.

One morning Martin was introduced to Pete Fields, a consultant, when visiting a supplier's office. Pete had worked with the supplier's management team and employees during the previous year to improve performance by improving their organizational effectiveness. Martin noted the supplier's openness to UVD's requirements and was impressed by the improved responsiveness he had experienced during this time.

Martin and John invited Pete to a meeting to discuss how performance improvement would help UVD.

Pete arrived early on the morning of the meeting but he only just made it to reception on time as he couldn't find a parking space anywhere in the UVD car park. Breathless, Pete stood at the front desk as he waited for the receptionist to finish on the telephone. After a few minutes, the receptionist looked up from her conversation and indicated that Pete should sign the guest book. When he was finished, the receptionist nodded him to a seat where Pete sat waiting to be taken to the meeting.

By the time Martin and John arrived to escort him into the meeting room, Pete had had a good opportunity to observe more employees of UVD as they hurried into work.

Following introductions, John briefed Pete on the company background. He then asked what Pete thought his services could provide for the company.

Pete looked directly at John and then Martin and said, "I am very impressed with what you have done with your business so far and how you arrived at this point. What I am not clear about is why you or your employees work so hard. Or why you would want to improve performance. What are you working for? What I hear about the future of UVD from what you've said sounds like more of what you have had in the past and that doesn't sound like it really inspires you."

John and Martin looked at each other sheepishly. Martin sighed and replied, "I'm embarrassed to say that it has really become just a job for me and I don't know why I do it anymore. Habit, I guess. Isn't that how it usually is? People join companies full of ideas but after a while they just get used to it."

"It doesn't have to be that way. I've seen many people and organizations get out of the kind of rut you are honest enough to describe – just by changing their practices – by substituting new habits for old," replied Pete. "The most important thing is that you want to make it happen. Do you?" asked Pete.

"Absolutely!" responded John. "It's what I've been trying to do, but I asked you here because I think I need a coach. It's so frustrating. I'm trying to drive and everyone keeps putting the brakes on!"

"Yes, EVERYONE puts the brakes on," interrupted Martin. They looked at Pete to continue.

Pete nodded and said, "OK, the first step in improving performance is articulating WHY you doing what you do. It may sound simplistic, but a shared vision or mission helps to direct energy in a focused way. But you might not be ready to create an aligned vision yet."

John shrugged his shoulders. "If I say what my vision is, I don't think I believe that we would ever stick to it, much less fulfill it. I know it sounds weak, but I don't think my staff is ready to do it. We have been through a lot together and it just isn't as easy to motivate people any more."

"Some CEOs take a day of convincing before they get to the clarity which you have just shown. The resistance comes from the fact that you and your team have a lot of history, John," said Pete. "We all make decisions and assumptions that shape the way that business looks to us based on our experiences, so we rarely look at something we know really well as if we are looking at it for the first time. Most management teams work in a swamp of old problems, issues and perceptions. Before you can create something new, you have to 'clear the swamp' of all the things you and your team already know about the business. I suggest that everyone at UVD go through a process of clearing the swamp before defining an aligned vision that you can work on together. Draining the swamp and creating a vision is the first step towards creating a new Paradigm for working together in your team."

John and Martin looked at each other and nodded at each other with an expression which said: "Oh yeah? Prove it!"

Martin spoke for them both with a challenge, "If you can do that, we'll be impressed."

"I can't. You can." answered Pete. "I can coach and support you, just as you can coach and support your team. When the rubber hits the road, it will be you and them that make it work. I can help you to take the brakes off UVD, but it's up to you to grab the steering wheel and start driving. It's always down to the management team to make it happen, and it is often confronting for them to do what is needed."

Martin nodded, "I guess that's us!"

Challenged, John smiled and looked at Pete and then at Martin, saying, "It sounds like a game worth playing. What do we need to do? What would you say I need to face up to?" By this time, John, Martin and Pete were excited.

Pete replied, "Your job is to lead. To believe there is a way even when you can't see it. To let it go when you feel like throttling one of your team and to know that anything that works is down to you and anything that doesn't work is down to you, too."

John and Pete had several subsequent meetings, in between which John was asked to clear his own swamp of issues and concerns and to create a vision of what was possible for his team and his business. Over time, he found himself getting more excited. The brakes seemed to be coming off - for him at least. Pete coached him ready to facilitate the first session with his whole management team.

John arranged the management team meeting. He was nervous. It was the first time he had actually brought the team together for such an important conversation. John introduced Pete as the meeting facilitator, describing his impressive track record to build credibility with his team – he knew how difficult they could be to impress.

John cleared his throat and began, "I'll hand over to Pete. He will explain the kind of work he has done with other companies and the kind of work we'll be doing, because today we are going to participate in a unique event at UVD. Over to you, Pete."

*Pete provided context for the meeting, "In my work with organizations, I have found that high performing organizations are high performing because they manage to articulate a vision **and** to implement that vision."*

He drew two axes on a flip chart.

"A vision answers the question WHAT are we going to do. Implementation is about HOW we are going to do it. Most organizations find it easy to create a vision but much harder to implement it. When we fail to implement a vision, we give up on it. We avoid talking about vision and work becomes monotonous. No one wants to work for an organization with no vision, but no one wants to feel like they are failing in implementing their vision. You have a lot going for you at UVD. John has set my goal for working with you. My goal in working with you is to help you to make this an organization that you are all proud of."

"To do this, you will create a shared vision and a shared plan. A shared vision has to excite you - so it's you that will create it. The problem is that, if you are anything like the other teams I've worked with, you've had your challenges in the past and you've learned some tough lessons. Every day you cross a 'swamp full of alligators' to do your jobs. That swamp is full of debris from everything that went wrong in the past. We need to clear away the debris of the past so we can create a vision for the future. Actually, even when we've cleared the debris, we're going to find some alligators in there – the real business issues you are dealing with. So to begin at the beginning, let's drain the swamp. What are all the issues and problems which stop UVD from being a great place to work and an effective organization. John, do you want to say anything before we continue?"

John spoke, "After today's meeting, I guarantee that each of us will begin to tap into a new creative energy around our work. How are we going to accomplish this? We are going to put to rest any niggles, resentments and complaints, we are going to say things that we have been putting off saying and anything else that has been blocking our enjoyment or effectiveness at work... even if it's me!"

"You are probably wondering why we are doing this. Martin and I see that it is possible to have a company that is driven by a vision. A company where the whole team helps to create the vision and contribute to its fulfillment. We know that UVD's success is due to you and we want to give you the opportunity to recreate UVD with us."

"We know you are all committed to the success of UVD. But what are we ALL working toward? Oh, I know that each of us could give a vague answer but what we are looking to create is an organization where we ALL feel we have a part to play. But before we can create a vision, there may be attitudes, disappointments, niggles, complaints or resentments that need to be cleared away first. Once we have completed this exercise we will be a place where, quite literally, we will be creating what we are about as a company newly."

"This is a safe space to say anything so we can all move forward. Who would like to go first?"

The management team who had initially squirmed in their seats uncomfortably were now sitting forward attentively. This sounded different!

Mark Jones, Manager of Manufacturing, cleared his throat and began, "Well, Manufacturing was put under a lot of stress by the late design revisions and, I know this for sure, that the team is very demoralized right now."

"But, we couldn't send out faulty...," replied John.

"Whoa," interrupted Pete. "A ground rule of a 'swamp clearing' meeting is that no one needs to defend anything. No one has done anything wrong. In fact, everyone is responding perfectly given the environment in which they have been working. If there are any really sticky points, then we can list them and make sure that something is done to rectify them. For now, just listen and list."

Mark and John both breathed a sigh of relief.

Several weeks later, after several swamp clearing sessions with all managers facilitated by consultant Pete Fields, the new mission of UltraViolet Design was formulated. The mission could only be created when everyone let go of his or her preconceived ideas about UVD.

The mission captures the spirit of innovation, accomplishment and making-a-difference that united the entire company, it is:

To be the #1 supplier of eco-friendly, designer products to leading furniture, department and specialist stores

Figure 2.5 UltraViolet Design's mission

After the mission was created, the strategic goals of UVD were identified:

- ▪ **Establish an ecologically sound image**
  A key to growth was identified as establishing an ecologically sound image. This is important to UVD for two reasons.
  First, new legislation in The Netherlands pertaining to waste management meant that all manufacturers, retailers/distributors and consumers must contribute to the disposal of products. The Dutch Government would probably take the lead in determining the European environmental legislation, which would need to be effective in all European countries within the next six years. In this respect, by producing ecologically sound products, UVD could gain a

competitive advantage, since most companies were not yet taking advantage of the marketing potential provided by the new legislation - and it would reduce the costs of waste disposal.

Second, when customers purchased UVD products in markets where the new legislation had not yet taken effect, would they need to associate UVD's slightly more expensive products with their eco-friendliness. When customers buy UVD products, they are buying into a lasting planet.

- ***Create international coverage***

    In order to be in a strong position for future growth and to achieve at least a minimum value of sales in each country, UVD wanted to deliver to the majority of stores in selected regions in each country. National coverage would strengthen their position as the number 1 supplier and would increase customer familiarity with UVD's products.

    In the US, coverage would be obtained by using the Internet, with distribution from a central warehouse. In the US, UVD would be 'going virtual'.

- ***Enhance Customer Satisfaction***

    In order to keep current customers and obtain new ones, customer satisfaction was seen as an important goal. Satisfied customers were loyal customers who would repeat business and, in addition, would provide UVD with free, word–of-mouth advertising.

- ***Increase profitability***

    As in all commercial organizations, being profitable was a necessity for the continuity of UVD. It would also be necessary to fund the considerable Research and Development (R&D) activities of the company, particularly in the expanding eco-friendly product range.

- ***Be innovative***

    To stay competitive UVD products would need to provide something that none of the competitor's products did.

In the crowded retail marketplace, innovation would be important in terms of design, features and functionality.

Another key area of innovation was the company's US marketing, which would leverage Web marketing, ordering and out-sourced warehousing and delivery.

- **Produce high-quality products**

     In order to gain and retain customers in the top tier of the retail market, the production of high-quality products was considered vital.

When Helen Case joined UVD recently as the new Chief Financial Officer (CFO), she immediately started with the improvement of the performance management and management reporting processes at UVD. The information UVD managers had at that time was mainly financial, very detailed, and everybody had difficulty reading and understanding the badly laid out printouts from the financial system. Hardly any Production or Marketing information was available and the management team had no Customer information at all. Also, the new Sales channel and Internet activity was hardly represented in the management information. Helen's aim was to implement a performance management process which UVD management could rely on for decision making and action taking.

We will follow John and Helen on their journey to establish a high-quality performance management process.

Section 2: The Habits

3. HABIT 1: DELIVER ON THE STRATEGY AND THE GOALS

KEY POINTS

☑ To be effective, the people in an organization must work in alignment.

☑ The strategic implementation process needs to be focused on value-creation, resulting in action, based on internal and external data and affecting the long-term view.

☑ To measure and manage long-term success, a balanced set of measures is required. Lagging information (like turnover, margin, cost and economic profit) needs to be combined with leading information (like customer perception, efficiency of processes and development of human capital). This is the basis of a Balanced Scorecard.

☑ The Financial, Customer, Process, and Personnel Development perspectives of the Balanced Scorecard are broken down into critical success factors and key performance indicators that measure success.

☑ To monitor achievement of their strategy, organizations must have information related to their strategy and goals.

The need for alignment

"You don't inform, you over-inform. ...Real communication takes time, and top management must be willing to make the investment."

Percy Barnevik, ABB

A central theme of the New Economy is 'speed'. Speed of innovation, speed of time-to-market, speed of execution. In order for an organization to satisfy this need for speed, all the people in the organization have to be aligned and working together. Everybody must know what the organization stands for, where it is going and what their own role is. The performance management process plays an important part in creating and maintaining alignment. The process can show and has to show whether strategic objectives are being achieved and whether value is being created. Corporate strategy must be translated into tangible objectives for all organizational levels so that everyone knows what the organization is aiming for. If there is a top-level, corporate strategy, there must be sub-strategies that make the strategy actionable at lower levels. To be effective overall, strategy at all levels must be aligned.

To make organizations, departments and teams work effectively, managers have to align and co-ordinate their activities. The reality is usually that different people within the same organization are pushing in different directions. Everyone may be working hard, and they may even be working smart, but only within the boundaries of what they see as important. The important question is: is the organization working smart?

An organization is working smart when everyone is doing what they need to do in order to implement the strategy - there is synergy between the actions of different individuals, teams, departments and business units. But how can an understanding of the strategy and the possibilities for synergy be communicated across the organization? And how can that strategy and synergy then be turned into action?

Here is a useful analogy. Iron is magnetic. But in an unmagnetized iron bar there are lots of tiny magnets, all pointing in different directions. The iron bar as a whole, therefore, has no resultant magnetic field. When a strong magnetic field is applied to the bar, all of the tiny magnets align themselves with the field. Even when the magnetic field is removed, most of the tiny magnets remain in alignment and the previously unmagnetized iron bar now has a magnetic field of its own.

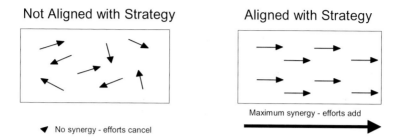

Figure 3.1: The power of alignment

By analogy, the magnetized iron bar can be compared with an organization that is working smarter, where everyone's actions are aligned with the strategy. So what is the strong magnetic field which magnetizes or aligns a whole organization?

To align an organization with strategy takes clear articulation and communication of the vision and strategy and ensuring that people then deliver on this strategy. It also takes an efficient infrastructure, consisting of a performance management process and information systems that monitor performance against the strategy and that keep everyone informed at all times. Critical success factors and key performance indicators measure performance against strategy and goals. Implementing strategy also requires the ability to identify exceptions and correct divergences from target to keep the organization on track. The Habits, 'Manage by Exception' and 'Manage by Action', look at this in detail.

The force field that really aligns and unifies an organization comes from its shared purpose, mission, vision and values. The next Habit, 'Create and Manage Internal Partnership', is about creating and managing this force field. But first, we give a simple overview of the ideas behind the Balanced Scorecard and take a deeper look into translating an organization's mission and strategy into metrics to measure and steer by.

Leading and lagging indicators

Financial measures may show if strategy was achieved in the past, but they don't show if it *will be* achieved in the future. Running an organization by monitoring only financial measures is like driving a car by looking in the rear view mirror. Financial measures that show what happened in the past are called **lagging indicators**. So, what can we measure and monitor to look out of the front windscreen, to anticipate problems before they happen? What does a **leading indicator** look like?

Often, these leading indicators are expressed in the form of critical success factors and key performance indicators. A critical success factor (CSF) provides a qualitative description of an element of the strategy in which the organization has to excel in order to be successful. A key performance indicator (KPI) is the way in which a critical success factor is measured. The use of critical success factors and key performance indicators enables measurement, and thus control, of strategic objectives. If performance indicators that measure the execution of the strategy are not included in the performance management process, it will not be clear whether strategic objectives are being achieved.

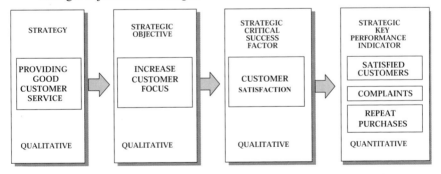

Figure 3.2: An example of a critical success factor and its accompanying key performance indicators

Providing good customer service is of critical importance for an organization's success. One of the ways to provide this service is by increasing the focus on the customer throughout the organization and thereby increasing customer satisfaction. Whether customer service is satisfactory is reflected in the number of customers that repeatedly buy products or services (*'repeat purchases'*). Customer satisfaction can also be measured by directly asking customers what they think of the services provided (*'satisfied customers'*). An important activity that helps to keep customers satisfied is to respond quickly to complaints. After all, making mistakes is inevitable, but correcting them as quickly as possible is not (*'complaint processing time'*).

The Balanced Scorecard is frequently used to present the financial and non-financial performance indicators in a user-friendly format. Traditionally, a Balanced Scorecard has four perspectives, or areas, which are monitored: innovation of products/services and people (including learning and growth of people), effectiveness of processes, experience of customers and financial performance. So which are the most leading of the leading indicators? To make a potentially complex subject simple, we can presume that there is a **cause and effect chain** between these perspectives, for example:

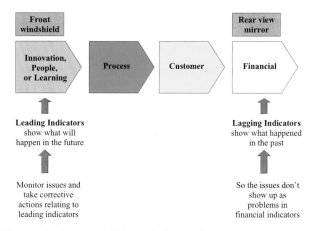

Figure 3.3: Cause and Effect in Balanced Scorecard Perspectives

- The **Innovation** perspective measures, for example, how often an organization introduces new products, services or (production) techniques. In this way, the organization makes sure it does not become complacent but continously renews itself. Some organizations replace or augment this perspective with a **People** perspective. It then measures the well being, commitment and competence of people in the organization. The People perspective measures cultural qualities (like internal partnership, teamwork, knowledge-sharing), as well as aggregate individual qualities (like leadership, competency, and use of technology).

- The **Process** perspective measures the effectiveness of the processes by which the organization creates value. It follows the People perspective because people impact the ability of the organization to create value by implementing and managing effective processes. The Process perspective measures how effectively processes operate. It precedes the Customer perspective because renewal of processes makes it possible for an organization to stay or become more competitive.

- The **Customer** perspective measures performance in terms of how the customer experiences the value created by the organization. It follows the Process perspective because value created by processes is only meaningful when it is perceived by the customer. The Customer perspective measures the value propositions that the organization delivers to its customers.

- The **Financial** perspective measures the 'bottom line', such as growth, return on investment and the other traditional measures of business performance. It is the last perspective because it is the final result of good, committed people, implementing and operating effective processes and creating value which customers have chosen to pay for. It looks to the results already achieved and is therefore a 'lagging perspective'.

In different organizations, the leading indicators are different, but the idea of a Balanced Scorecard is to *combine* lagging and leading indicators to give an understanding of where the organization is *and* where it is going. Different organizations also choose different perspectives, but the principle is the same, a 'balanced' set of measures that allow an organization to measure the cause and effect chain by which customer and shareholder value is created. If value is created by people working on and in processes, to satisfy customers and produce financial results, then managers must be able to measure and monitor all of these perspectives of value-creation to effectively manage.

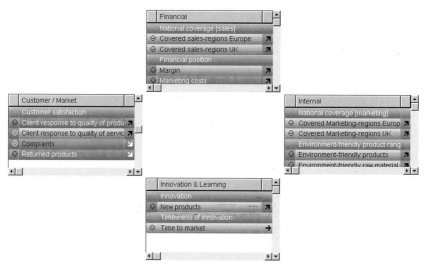

Figure 3.4: Example of a Balanced Scorecard

Figure 3.4 gives a top-level overview of the four perspectives of a Balanced Scorecard. For each of the four perspectives, it shows:

- actual performance in the centre column (colours: red, yellow and green),

- the change compared to history in the left hand column (indicators: ☺, ☺, and ☹, with traffic light colouring) and

- the expected future performance in the right hand column (indicators: ↗,→ and ↘, with traffic light colouring to indicate the expected future state).

Here are a few examples of why it is necessary to measure leading indicators.

- Most organizations state that **People** are their main asset. Reporting on the number of full-time employees and absenteeism is not enough. Managers need insight into the commitment, quality, motivation and satisfaction level of personnel in order to make meaningful human resource decisions.

- **Customer** satisfaction and the needs of customers must be continually and systematically monitored in order to anticipate future behaviour and continue to deliver satisfaction and value. Quality, timeliness and added value of delivered products or services must be continuously evaluated.

- The organization's ability to **Innovate** and to adapt to change must be monitored. Because these abilities are crucial for the organization to survive in a changing world. Poor performance in these areas may only show up in the financials after a significant time-delay. By that time the opportunity for action or correction may have been missed.

The main benefit of managing with a combination of financial and non-financial information is that the use of leading, non-financial indicators facilitates pro-active control and the ability to take preventative action. A balanced set of key financial and non-financial indicators enables management to focus on the really important issues that drive business performance and to monitor the achievement of strategic goals more closely. Using non-financial information improves analysis capabilities because management can identify the root causes of financial performance. The non-financials can include external information, making it possible for management to compare the internal results with external trends and drivers.

In summary, in order to make the performance management process more relevant to the organization's strategy, managers have to first formulate clear objectives that are derived from the strategy. These strategic objectives make the strategy more tangible, when they are measured by means of critical success factors and key performance indicators. In a large organization, on the basis of the strategic objectives, objectives may be formulated for each division and department. These objectives may then also be translated into critical success factors and key performance indicators. As performance is measured, action plans are created based on the actual values of the critical success factors and key performance indicators compared to pre-set targets. The management of these objectives, critical success factors, key performance indicators and action plans is a way to steer the organization to achieve its strategy.

Developing critical success factors and key performance indicators

This section describes a detailed process for developing critical success factors and key performance indicators at all levels. You may wish to skip it at first reading and come back to it when you need to develop indicators for your organization. Although the process is described in a top-down way, in practice, the need for creative input and personal commitment from managers and employees is leading to organizations replacing top-down imposition of strategy with collaborative, iterative development of strategy. (See Habit 2, Levels of Participation, Commitment and Purpose.)

The development of critical success factors and key performance indicators is at the center of many improvement projects for the performance management process. In this section, the development process of these measures is described using the Performance Measurement Pyramid.

Figure 3.5: The Performance Measurement Pyramid

The Performance Measurement Pyramid is made up of:

- *Mission and strategy.* First of all, an organization has to formulate its mission by answering the question '*What* do we, as an organization, want to accomplish – our mission?' To formulate a strategy, an organization has to answers the questions, '*How* are we as an organization going to achieve our mission?' and '*How* can we accomplish what we want?'

  Suppose an organization has the following mission: to double in size, while retaining a socially conscious image. Possible strategies for achieving such a mission might be: to make the organization focus more on customer satisfaction, to develop new eco products and to sponsor local environmental projects.

- *Strategic objectives, critical success factors and key performance indicators.* In order to make an organization's strategy tangible, strategic objectives need to be formulated. A strategy is often expressed in abstract terms. By formulating one or more strategic objectives, it becomes clear which activities have to be undertaken in order to implement the organization's strategy. If the strategy is already expressed in specific, measurable terms, an organization's strategy and its strategic objectives are virtually the same.

Whether strategic objectives are being achieved can be monitored with strategic critical success factors and measured with strategic key performance indicators. (See Figure 3.2 for an example). These strategic measures are included in the management reporting that is used by the organization's Board of Directors or management team. Often, the Balanced Scorecard of an organization is composed of these strategic measures. For an organization with diverse activities, a complete Balanced Scorecard on the corporate level may not be meaningful because the non-financial indicators cannot be meaningfully aggregated across subsidiary businesses. In that case, only a limited number of financial indicators are reported in a Key Value Driver summary.

- *Functional objectives, critical success factors and key performance indicators.* A business function or department can support an organization's mission and strategy by translating the strategic objectives into their own functional area by defining functional objectives for that business function or department. The extent to which the functional objectives are achieved is monitored with functional critical success factors and measured with functional key performance indicators. These functional measures are used particularly by managers of various functional disciplines or middle managers. These functional measures can be included in a Balanced Scorecard for the department or can be represented as a

Key Value Driver overview without necessarily having to make a complete Balanced Scorecard.

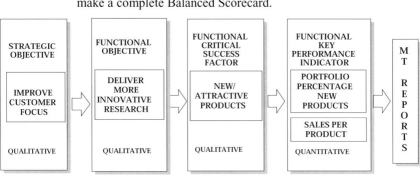

Figure 3.6: Functional critical success factors and key performance indicators (for the R&D department)

Suppose the Research & Development department of an organization translates the strategic objective 'Improve customer focus' into the functional objective of 'conducting more innovative research'. After all, the more products that are developed that meet the customer's demands, the more satisfied the customer will be. It is critical to the R&D department, therefore, to monitor whether the department succeeds in developing enough new products which are also attractive to customers. Whether customers appreciate these new products can be measured using turnover of new products. Whether the number of new products developed is sufficient can be measured on the basis of the share that these new products have in the product portfolio.

Because every business function or department contributes in its own way to the achievement of strategic objectives, it is essential to determine the functional objectives for each business function or department separately. Management has the responsibility to continuously monitor whether the functional objectives and the strategic objectives are aligned. If this is not the case, or is no longer the case, the functional objectives need to be reformulated. This is an effective way for the organization to maintain alignment.

- *Crucial business activities, operational critical success factors and key performance indicators.* In addition to the mission and strategy, every organization has specific crucial business activities. We define a crucial business activity as an activity 'that makes the business tick' and, for this reason, must *always* be executed in order for the business to survive, regardless of the chosen mission. The execution of crucial business activities is *monitored* by means of operational critical success factors and *measured* with operational key performance indicators. These operational measures are used particularly by managers who are directly involved in the crucial business activities. These operational measures can also be included in the Balanced Scorecard for the department or they can be represented as a Key Value Driver overview without having to make a complete Balanced Scorecard.

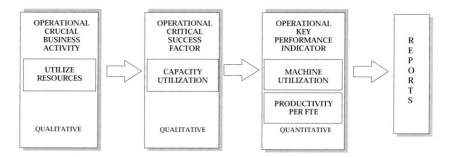

Figure 3.7: Operational critical success factors and key performance indicators

Suppose an organization has to make optimal use of its assets to prevent product costs becoming too high. If the organization's strategy is 'to bring high-quality consumer products to the market at a low price' it may well occur that high-quality products are indeed available for the desired (low) selling price. But if the organization does not watch the costs, they are likely to become too high, resulting in a profit margin that is too small for the organization to be able to continue investing properly. The continuity of the organization will be in danger despite the organization's successful implementation of its strategy. In addition to machine capacity, personnel capacity can be measured as well, for example by calculating the productivity per FTE (Full Time Equivalent).

- *Environmental factors and environmental key performance indicators.* These are measures that provide information on the environment in which an organization operates, and especially on developments that are relevant to the organization. It concerns measures that can be controlled partly or not at all by the organization but at the same time have an effect on the results of the organization. This is why, especially during the target-setting process for key performance indicators, managers have to take into account the influence of environmental factors. These business environment measures can be included as an extra perspective in the Balanced Scorecard of the organization.

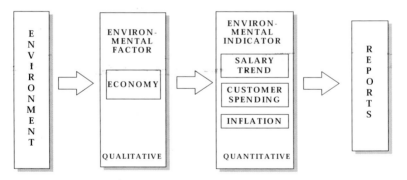

Figure 3.8: Environmental factors and environmental key performance indicators

Economic developments usually have a direct influence on an organization's business results and are, therefore, critical to the organization's success. Many indicators, such as salary and wage developments, inflation (and interest rates) and the accompanying consumer spending indices, provide important input for estimating, among other measures, the expected turnover. If the economy grows more slowly than initially expected, the targeted sales budget can be adjusted downwards. If, even then, the sales manager does not succeed in realizing the adjusted target, the most obvious explanation ('We had a downward economic trend') cannot be used and thus the manager has to look for the *real* causes of not achieving the target.

During the development process of key performance indicators, a distinction should be made between what is *management* information and what is *operational* information.

Figure 3.9: The relationship between management information and operational information

Operational information gives an overview of the individual activities within the organization. Operational information enables an organization to decide which activities should be redirected or adjusted and which follow-up steps should be taken, showing the consequences in time and money. The process indicators that are used in operational information should not be included in management reporting. Process indicators are usually gleaned from detailed operational data that generally becomes available after an activity has been finished or finalized. An example of a process indicator is 'the delivery time of a *single* order'.

Management information, based on critical success factors and key performance indicators, is information that is generated at a higher, more abstract level than operational information. Management information has a signalling function, informing management if a certain process is heading in the right direction or not, and if performance is in accordance with agreements and targets that have been made previously. The operational key performance indicators that are used in management information are often compiled of process indicators. Management information reporting is produced periodically, usually once a month. If managers have not achieved their targets, management generally asks for an analysis of the underlying causes for the failure. For this reason, the operational data that was mentioned earlier needs to be accessed in an ad hoc manner. An example of an operational key performance indicator that consists of process indicator data is 'the *average* delivery time of orders'. Value Based Management seeks to measure all of the activities of an organization in terms of the value which they create. (For a description of how the Balanced Scorecard can be used with Value Based Management, see Appendix F.)

Case Study: Developing performance indicators and a Balanced Scorecard for UltraViolet Design

At the next meeting Pete Fields addressed the management team of UVD, who had been listening intently to his explaination of Critical Success Factors and Key Performance Indicators.

"What is the starting-point when you want to develop Critical Success Factors?" he asked.

John Williams took the lead. "Mission and strategy."

"That's right. We determined these over the past few weeks. What were they again?"

"The mission we formulated was that we, as a company, want to become the most prominent supplier of eco-friendly, designer products in the market segments of the top furniture stores, department stores and specialist stores," Gary Williams summed up.
"And how are you going to achieve this?" was Pete's next question.

"We are going to accomplish our mission through establishing an environmentally-friendly image, supported by high quality products," interjected Martin. *"And we want to create international coverage by constantly being the first to introduce innovative and high-quality products to the market, while at the same time enhancing customer satisfaction with our products."*

"And this should all result in increased customer satisfaction and profitability for UltraViolet Design," added John quickly.

To which Jeannette added, *"Let's not forget the Web presence as being very important for our eBusiness!"*

"Very good", said Pete, as he wrote down the Strategic Objectives on a flipchart. *"Now we have to derive the Critical Success Factors for these Strategic Objectives. Which matters are of utmost importance to UltraViolet Design so that we have to constantly monitor them? First, let's take an easy one - the image, for example. What Strategic Actions could we formulate for it?"*

"What exactly do you mean by strategic action?" asked Gary.

Before Pete had a chance to, Helen answered, *"In order to be able to execute the strategy we have to design outcomes to fulfill each of the Strategic Objectives. And in order to monitor the progress of these actions, we need Key Performance Indicators."*

"Could you give an example?" Martin asked.

"Look at image," Helen continued. *"We want to distinguish ourselves from our competitors by using the eco-friendly image of our products to sell more products. The outcome we need is a positive image which makes customers turn to UVD instead of the competition."*

"Why?" asked Pete.

"Well," replied Helen, *"we currently use highly-priced, and I still believe much too highly-priced, recyclable raw materials in our*

products because we are extremely aware of the effect of manufacturing on the environment. We need to communicate our commitment to the environment to our customers, otherwise we can't really justify our high prices compared to the competition."

She took a deep breath before continuing. "Another reason to pursue an environment-friendly image is that the end-consumer may turn away from our products because they are not aware that they do not contain plastics, which are generally known to be bad for the environment. Our clients, the retailers, would no longer buy our products and we would end up with a warehouse full of goods that are too highly priced."

"How would you translate this into a Critical Success Factor?" Pete asked.

Helen replied, "I think that our first Critical Success Factor would be an environment-friendly image."

Pete quickly wrote this down on the flipchart. "I agree with you. If UltraViolet Design doesn't keep a close eye on image, you will never be able to execute the company's strategy."

"But," Gary interjected, "how can you measure this Critical Success Factor, then?"

Pete replied, "That's a good question, Gary. You can measure environment-friendly image, the first Critical Success Factor, with the aid of a Key Performance Indicator. We'll figure that out later today. We are purposely detaching identifying the issues that are of strategic importance to the company from the measures for those issues. We do this because otherwise we run the risk of identifying and using only a single indicator, whereas a Critical Success Factor may well be defined and monitored by multiple Key Performance Indicators. If you delve into detail too soon, you will lose your overview. We discuss measures later on. Does this make sense?"

"I understand," Gary nodded. "So, what are the other Critical Success Factors?"

The group worked enthusiastically and Pete was able to enter a comprehensive list of Critical Success Factors into his laptop computer.

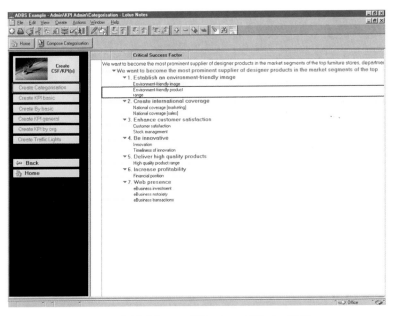

Figure 3.10: Mission, Objectives, CSFs for UVD

After lunch, Pete kicked off the meeting again. "This afternoon we are going to determine which Key Performance Indicators can measure the Critical Success Factors we created this morning. We will also think about ways to find the data that is needed for the Key Performance Indicators. This is going to be exciting! I guarantee that you will not want an after-lunch nap! John, would you do the honours and get us started?"

John jumped up out of his chair: "Let's start with the first Critical Success Factor, 'the environment-friendly image'. It seems logical to me that if you want to find out how the market views you, you go out and investigate that in some way."

"What do you think about asking for our clients' reactions?" said Martin, putting in his bit.

John gave his brother a questioning look, "What do you mean?"

"Well, we can conduct a client survey in which we ask our clients about our image. For example, how they view us, whether they feel that we make environment-friendly products or not, or whether they have an opinion at all. If they don't, then we have some work to do on our image!" Martin replied thoughtfully.

John commented, "Sounds good. So the key performance indicator is 'client responses'. We want to know the number of positive client responses as compared to the total of all client responses. We can measure that with a special survey."

"Or, we make this a continuous survey so that we can see the number of positive responses per period," said Martin enthusiastically.

Helen commented, "Wait a minute, Martin. Do you have any idea what it costs to carry out these surveys continually? Money doesn't grow on trees here – trust me, I know!"

Jeanette came to Martin's aid. "But, Helen, we just decided that image is crucial for UltraViolet Design's success. Having decided that, we have to accept the consequences as well as the rewards. We cannot put our faith in random signals from the market or from our clients. We will have to conduct a structured survey."

Helen nodded and Jeanette went on, "Yes, this could be rather expensive, particularly if you've never done it before and still have to set everything up. But think, just for a second, about the alternative: being in the dark about information that is of great importance to our company. We'll never be able to direct anything, let alone redirect anything!"

Jeanette put Helen's mind at ease. "Of course, you can look for a inexpensive alternative for the measurement method. Just as long as we get the results somehow."

"In that case," commented Gary flippantly, "we could use spot-check surveys to ask if our clients have any complaints about the quality of our products."

"Excellent idea," commented John. *"This data can then be included with the complaints that we currently capture in our sales system."*

"I still have a question about this, Pete," Martin said. *"In principle, you use this key performance indicator to monitor how the image of our products is doing in the market. This will also enable us to take action, based on the key performance indicator's progress, if things are not going well. Do you have a suggestion about how we can influence our image positively?"*

"Are you familiar with the green 'eco-sticker' which they use in Germany?" Pete answered. *"You could consider putting a sticker on your products so that the consumer sees that this product is environmentally friendly. I think some supermarket introduced something similar last year in Europe."*

Gary was the first to respond. *"That's what I was thinking of. In any case it means that we should support the environment-friendly image with an environment-friendly range. We now have a number of environment-friendly products, but we don't really know what percentage of the entire product portfolio they represent. We will have to monitor that as well."*

"And how would you go about measuring that?" Pete asked.

Gary brightened, *"We could extract that information from our product database."*

The group worked happily while Pete entered the Key Performance Indicators into his laptop.

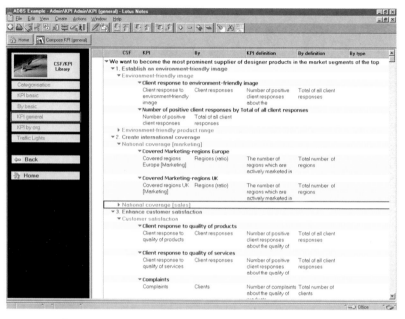

Figure 3.11: Mission, Objectives, CSFs and Kpis for UVD

Pete Fields felt quite content as he looked back on the long and productive day. He summarized the progress for the group, "Well done, you have achieved a lot today. You were able define Critical Success Factors. And I am especially happy that you have been able to define some important eMeasures with which to measure your new distribution channel, the Internet! The important thing to remember is that this is an iterative process. Review it once or twice a year and you will always be right on top of the most important developments in your company!"

"The Critical Success Factors and Key Performance Indicators must be included in the Balanced Scorecard of UltraViolet Design. This means that, in addition to regular financial reports, you will now work with the Scorecard in your new Action Driven Balanced Scorecard system, ADBS. You have to interface the ADBS

with the operational and supporting information systems to calculate the Key Performance Indicators. In addition to this, you also need to initiate some new procedures including customer surveys."

John stood up and grinned as he spoke, "There's enough to do then!"

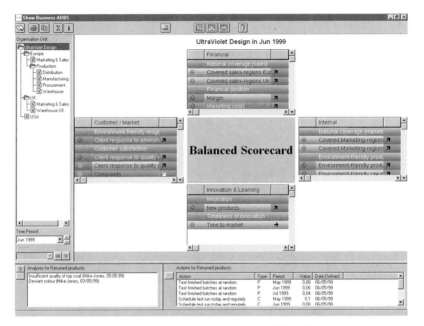

Figure 3.12: The Balanced Scorecard for UVD

He shook Pete's hand, "Pete, on behalf of everyone, I'd like to thank you for your help. We're going to make this work!"

The Williams brothers, Helen Case and Jeannette Barrymoor nodded in agreement and left the meeting room discussing the events of the past two days with great animation.

4. HABIT 2: CREATE AND MANAGE INTERNAL PARTNERSHIP

KEY POINTS

☑ Internal partnership is a powerful ingredient for organizational effectiveness and rapid change.

☑ Invest in creating and maintaining a Paradigm of internal partnership.

☑ Listen to people's issues and concerns before trying to get buy-in.

☑ To achieve maximum commitment, co-create and co-own the strategy.

☑ Create a vision that is 'big enough' to encompass the vision of each person in the organization.

☑ People are most effective when they are working on something consistent with their own purpose.

☑ Create partnership from Purpose to Vision to Plan to Action.

☑ Manage internal partnership when changing the performance management process.

The need for Internal Partnership

The New Economy is characterized by speed and enabled by unprecedented accessibility of information. Skills, knowledge and experience, which were traditionally the domain of a select few, are now available to everyone. The speed with which competitive strategies are adopted across a sector is increasing, leveling the playing field and forcing new strategies to be identified and deployed more and more rapidly. The difference between winners and losers in this revolution is the ability of the organization to implement strategy. Harnessing the collective motivation, drive and creativity of the entire workforce is key to effective implementation. Processes and technology can be copied. The culture that distinguishes partnership and co-operation in one organization from politics and bureaucracy in another is a vital determinant of success.

The people challenge of high performance is, therefore, to create internal partnership and to capture and sustain the energy of a group of people, so that they work hard and smart towards shared goals. Great organizations are built on good people working with vision, drive and enthusiasm. Characteristics of good internal partnership include:

- people sharing their knowledge and information for the good of the organization;

- people giving up fixed positions when those positions do not create value for the team;

- people behaving like owners of the organization, rather than employees or on-lookers;

- people creating solutions, rather than excuses based on politics, bureaucracy and protocol;

- the focus is on results, (outcomes), rather than inputs and outputs.

Internal partnership results *in* aligned effective actions from a team of people. Internal partnership results *from* alignment of Purpose, Vision and Plan within the group of people. Partnership is a Paradigm that underlies a relationship.

Internal Partnership has two sides: empowerment by the organization and responsibility of the employee. It requires a shift in relationship between the organization and the employee, a shift in Paradigm. Jack Walsh, CEO of General Electric, recognized this and is famous for saying: "Control your destiny or someone else will."

If our organizations do not do things better in the new millennium, than we did in the old, our long-term destiny does not look good. Today the challenge could be expressed with the question: 'If *we* don't control our destiny, who will?'

We need to create organizations that create value for stakeholders. We need to expand our definition of stakeholders to include the society and environment in which our organizations operate. Fundamentally, executives, managers and front-line employees know this, so to ignore the fact inhibits commitment and performance. The ultimate motivation is to know that by doing our work, we are paying the bills and doing something worthwhile.

Managing Paradigm

The ability to manage the Paradigm through which people perceive a situation is a vital leadership skill in times of change or uncertainty. In times of change, the Paradigm of partnership is most vulnerable and it is most vital to the organization if change is to be successful. How do we manage the Paradigm? First, we have to become aware of its existence, then we have to learn to consciously track and manage it.

Some time ago, we consulted on performance management for a newly acquired division of a multinational that has a proven track record of high performance across the multiple sectors in which it operates. The purpose of the performance management system was not for exercising strategic control, but for empowerment of every employee within the business. They did not so much want to inform management, as to involve every employee. Over time, we learned that this was part of a consistent and unmistakable commitment to internal partnership: treating people as adults and, as a result, expecting and receiving extraordinary accountability and responsibility from happy enthusiastic people. This was not a long-established division where the relationship had developed over many years. It was a new acquisition where we saw the transformation of Paradigm from sceptical observation of the new management to complete partnership.

For this organization, the performance management system did not stop with management. Every member of every team knew their service level targets for every week. It was a 'game' and it was named and played as a game. Many programs and activities contributed to the unmistakable conclusion of employees that the organization was taking them seriously and was committed to the value of their contribution beyond the number of hours they worked.

This was a business that was winning for all of its stakeholders – including shareholders, employees and customers - a business able to deliver results by getting the most out of its people. Rather than internal partnership just supporting business processes, business processes and systems were created and maintained to create and maintain internal partnership.

Recently we encountered another example of the importance of Paradigm. We were presenting to a group of people from across the divisions of a multinational. Headquarters believed that a performance management portal would be a powerful tool to help the organization to deliver on its strategy. As such, they saw the system as desirable, if not essential. A presentation was set up to win the buy-in of the divisions.

Without awareness of Paradigm, we might have made the presentation of the benefits perceived by Headquarters. We would have grown increasingly uneasy at the body language of crossed arms and legs from the audience, communicating that there was a problem. To prevent this situation, we asked a question in advance, to find out the issues and concerns which might stop representatives of the divisions hearing what we had to say.

As one of our colleagues, Mike Griffiths, would say:

"If you want to fight the alligators, you have to drain the swamp."

What he means is, you have to allow all of the issues and concerns to be acknowledged before you can address the key business problems. If you do not hear people's concerns first, they are unlikely to hear what you really want to say.

We introduced our objective, which was to receive their input to an important decision. To 'drain the swamp' we asked them: "What are your concerns with this proposition and what opportunities do you see."

The feedback gave us a clear understanding of the Paradigm in which the divisions were holding the project. First, we heard issues relating to WHAT should be done and HOW it should be done: problems with technology, standards, and timescales. Underpinning all of these was a concern about WHY it was being done. For one division, it looked like a way to take away their independence and freedom to manage. They did not want enforced control from the Headquarters, so they would disagree with the WHAT and HOW of implementing and as a result block the project. As it happens, Headquarters was trying to save time and money for every division, to allow transparency of information across divisions, learning between divisions and a shift of Paradigm to internal partnership. That was not what the divisions perceived.

Headquarters was not **trusted** and hence was not **credible**, so no progress could be made even though the large financial and time-savings were relevant to every division. A long, painful negotiation was avoided by dealing with the issue of trust, by making sure that Headquarters and the divisions agreed on WHY the project was necessary. After draining the swamp, the real issue of trust was uncovered. It could then be dealt with, for example by:

- promising not to use the performance management infrastructure as a way to interfere with the divisions, but only to intervene in cases of agreed exceptions;

- allowing the divisions to control the security access to their own performance management systems;

- pointing out that the organization must have a performance management breakthrough if it was to survive market trends, and by providing credible proof of this.

Alternatively, Headquarters could mandate the tools and approach and postpone the buy-in issue. Executives sometimes have to take tough decisions. If, with hindsight, they are seen to have acted fairly and with a commitment to a win-win for employees and the business, then they are more likely to be trusted in future. The

Paradigm of internal partnership is enhanced and the executive has more power as a leader.

We can take some valuable lessons from this example:

- If achieving our goal requires commitment from others, it requires their buy-in.

- As a first step towards creating buy-in, we need to understand the Paradigm from which the other person or group is operating.

- Draining the swamp – actively exposing and acknowledging issues – can give us this understanding.

- If we expose and acknowledge these issues with respect and compassion, in order to understand, rather than to manipulate, then mutual understanding, trust and respect begins to be created.

- Draining the swamp allows us to identify the business, technical and people barriers to our goal.

- Draining the swamp allows us to identify the real alligators that we need to fight in order to achieve our goal.

- Often we fight imaginary alligators, assuming that people want intellectual justification of project plans in order to buy-in, when the real alligators are submerged concerns, for example about job security, power and control.

Internal Partnership describes a Paradigm, a place from which to come when communicating with people. It is not a tool or methodology. It is not a way of doing something or know-how. It is more a mind-set, or more accurately, a way of thinking shared by a team which shows itself in the mind-set and behaviour of the individuals in that team. Effective teamwork is the symptom. The Paradigm of internal partnership is the cause.

A Paradigm of internal partnership is the underpinning of any win-win relationship, whether the relationship is a marriage, a supplier-customer relationship, or a relationship between colleagues. A Paradigm of internal partnership allows issues and disagreements to be resolved quickly and effectively. Without the Paradigm of partnership, differences may be irreconcilable. The key insight is that underlying every relationship is a Paradigm

A Paradigm of partnership enables high-performance because both parties are working together for the same outcome, rather than competing, manipulating, or resisting to further a private agenda. The organization in which the Paradigm between employee and employer is win-win will be capable of more than the organization where the Paradigm for work is 'do as little as you can'. A manager who can create and maintain the Paradigm of partnership can get superhuman performance from her or his team. The good news is, as one of our colleagues, Rob Kendall, puts it:

"Paradigm is maleable. It can change in an instant."

The buy-in questions

First, a word of caution. Creating internal partnership is an emotional intelligence skill, rather than a technique. This means that it is most effectively learned through practice and can be accelerated in a facilitated workshop rather than in classroom training or from a book!

Let's start by looking at this at a one-to-one level. What does it take for me to create a Paradigm of partnership in my relationship with you?

You need to know that I am worthy of your partnership. For this, I must be trustworthy and credible. You need to know that I want what is best for you and will support you to achieve it or that we want things in common and will work together to achieve them. Let's be more specific to start with. If I want your partnership or your 'buy-in' to achieving my agenda, then what I want to achieve must be relevant to you. It must be worth *your* while to give your support.

In leading workshops and coaching change agents, (The Buy-in Workshop, Kendall and Fourman, 1996-1999), we have found that the following four, simple questions are powerful tools for creating buy-in and developing a Paradigm of partnership in relation to a specific project. It is not the answers to the questions that matter, so much as the shift of Paradigm that can occur when they are considered.

If you want buy-in from someone, they must answer each of the buy-in questions positively:

1. Is it credible?

When you know that the project is credible to the other person and that you are respected as trustworthy, you can go on. This was the question where we got stuck in the second example above. Headquarters was not credible because it was not trusted by the people in the divisions.

2. Is it relevant?

How does it relate to their purpose and objectives? Once they know that the project is relevant to them, you can go on.

3. Is it worth it?

Once they know that the value of the project to them outweighs the cost, you can go on.

4. WHAT action will you take now?

Buy-in is buy-in when there is action. This could be anything from sponsorship, to funding, to accepting accountability.

To know the power of these questions, you have to practice with them. Try it with your spouse, your children, or a colleague. If a conversation seems to be stuck, find out where by asking the questions above in order. When you find the blockage, address it. You may be surprised at how much stress this simple tool can eliminate and at how quickly you can unblock resistance to good win-win ideas. As you might expect, the buy-in questions do not work if you are trying to manipulate or control someone into doing something that is not really in their interest. Well, you don't really want that to be done to you either, do you?

Buy-in is a function of perception. It can change in an instant. When things change or expectations are not fulfilled, the Paradigm can shift - people get upset and where you had buy-in, you get resistance. The bad news is that you need to continue to manage buy-in, continue to manage and maintain the Paradigm of partnership. The good news is that managing Paradigm costs less time, money, effort and stress than trying to manage all the consequences of losing the Paradigm of partnership.

Levels of participation, commitment and purpose

"For this is the true joy in life, to be used by a
purpose recognised by yourself as a mighty one. Life
is no brief candle to me. It is a kind of splendid torch
which we have for a moment before passing on to
future generations. I want to be thoroughly used up
when I die."
George Bernard Shaw

The management of a team or organization determines how much participation employees have in creating the strategy. We can offer different levels of **participation** to a team, which will result in a different perception of whose 'game' we are playing:

- Delivering the strategy created by management – it is management's game: having the internal partnership of the people in the organization to deliver on the vision and the strategy.

- Co-creating the strategy – it is everyone's game: having the people in the organization as co-creators of the vision and the strategy, as well as partners in delivering the vision and strategy. Expect surprising insight, lateral thinking, intelligence and commitment.

With a Paradigm of internal Partnership, it does not matter who created the strategy because the people in the organization are partners. But co-creating the strategy is one way of tapping into the collective knowledge and insight of the people in the organization and of ensuring ownership.

There are also two levels of **commitment** which we can elicit from a team, depending whether we appeal to just their ambition to succeed in the organization, or to their purpose in life too:

- Appeal to ambition – measurement and rewards are the motivator: people will do what is needed to achieve rewards, but their motivation may dissolve when the rewards do not materialise. Rewards and incentives can be detrimental to long-term performance. They shift people from intrinsic motivation to extrinsic motivation. This in turn shifts their attention from doing a good job to doing a job in a way that will be rewarded well. Also, extrinsic motivation is like an addiction. It is satisfying at first, but it loses its power, and the rewards have to escalate to avoid disenchantment.

- Appeal to purpose – the organization allows the person to fulfill on their purpose: people will do what is needed because it has meaning and value to them. Expect commitment and heroism.

Combining participation in strategy development and motivation by purpose is a powerful tool for organisational leaders who want, or need, breakthrough results.

The Paradigm that we have for our work is as important to our satisfaction and results as the nature of the work itself. Let's consider an example:

> *Several hundred years ago, a young man was travelling, seeking his way in life. He came upon a stone quarry, which he passed to find a patch of muddy ground. Many people passed by him, each carrying stone. The young man came upon three men, each with a hammer and a chisel, working stone in a similar shape.*
>
> *He stopped and asked the first man: "Excuse me, sir. What are you doing?"*

The man looked up and replied: "Son, I'm hammering stone."

The young man asked: "And, sir, how do you find it, doing what you do?"

The man answered: "It's hard work when it rains like this, but at least it's a living."

"Thank you, sir," replied the young man.

He walked a few paces further and would have walked on, but the second man seemed to work with more interest. So the young man asked as he passed the second man: "Excuse me, sir. What are you doing?"

The man looked up with a faint smile and answered: "I'm building a Gothic arch."

The young man noticed the pride in the man's voice and asked: "And, sir, how do you find it, doing what you do?"

The second man answered: "I like what I do because there is always something to show for a day's work."

"Thank you, sir," replied the young man.

He walked a few paces further and would again have walked on, but the third man was different again. So the young man asked: "Excuse me, sir. What are you doing?"

For a moment it seemed the third man didn't hear him. Then he turned to reveal an intense expression on his face, which melted into a broad smile as he reflected on the young man's question. The third man spoke: "I'm building a beautiful cathedral which will stand long after you and I have passed by."

The young man felt deep admiration for this man who had passion in his voice and a tear in his eye working here in a field of mud. He asked: "Sir, how does it feel to do this work?"

The stone mason stood up, put his hand on the young man's shoulder and answered. "Some nights I dream of my cathedral. Every day I am building my dream. Sometimes I stay until the last light, just to complete one more arch, one more corner stone. I love this work."

The young man knew that he had found his way in life. His voice broke as he asked, "Sir, can you teach me to do what you do?"

The third stone mason created more value than the other two masons, but not because he was paid piece meal. The Paradigm in which he worked was different. The organization for which he worked had won his commitment and, with it, his discretionary effort - because for him, his work had purpose.

Doing work that matches our purpose is motivating and exhilarating. Is there any cost to the organization in having people do work which is not consistent with their principles?

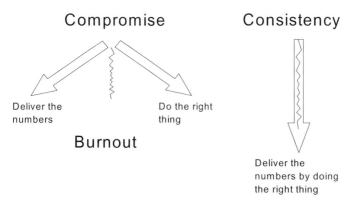

Figure 4.1: The benefit of consistency with principles

If a manager is continually compromising her or his own beliefs and values for that which delivers the numbers, the result is stress, de-motivation and burnout. In these circumstances, good people either leave or become resigned and cynical. This is because it is not just what we *do* that matters - it is what it *means* to us.

The rocket-ship analogy illustrates the power of allowing someone to do work which rewards their ambition to succeed in the organization and their personal purpose. When purpose and ambition are in alignment, the rocket is driven forward. When purpose and ambition are not in alignment, the rocket goes round in circles.

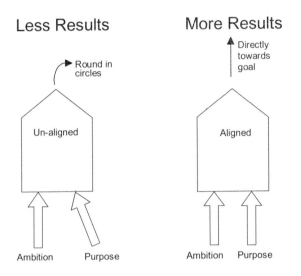

Figure 4.2: The importance of alignment of ambition with purpose

The manager's responsibility is to make sure that their own ambition and purpose are aligned with the mission, values, strategy and goals of the organization, and to facilitate this alignment for their team and not get in the way of their alignment. Without this alignment, it is hard to produce results.

There is a spiritual law attributed to an unknown Indian sage which says:

> *"The Universe denies us that which we most want*
> *[Ambition] in order to force us to attain that which we*
> *most need to grow and develop [Purpose]."*

To translate this into pragmatic terms: '*Managers will find it hard to achieve their goals unless what they are doing is consistent with their purpose.*'

To create an organization that brings out the greatness in people, we need to create an organization with a purpose recognized by its people as 'a mighty one'. The organization must have a purpose and vision that has personal meaning for each of its employees. If the organization's purpose fulfills or is aligned with the purpose of each of the individuals within it, they can all be 100% committed and, as a result, will find it easy to be motivated. This illustrates why it is valuable to *co-create* a purpose rather than simply to impose one from the top down.

WHY, WHAT and HOW

"If you have a company with itsy-bitsy vision, you have an itsy-bitsy company."

Anita Roddick
The Body Shop

As human beings, we seem to have an in-built resistance to change, which makes life challenging for the would-be change agent. Worse than that, when we resist change, we are often not honest about WHY we are resisting it. Sometimes we are not even aware of WHY we are resisting it. So, for the would-be change agent, learning to listen for and identify someone else's reason WHY is a vital skill. It is another example of Paradigm.

If a team is arguing about WHAT has to be done or HOW to do it, this may just be a symptom of the concern that they have about WHY it is being done. Individuals and groups will resist ideas based on any conflict with their personal agenda, motivation, or reason WHY. If there is no alignment on WHY the change is happening, it will be hard (or impossible) to reach agreement on WHAT or HOW it will be done. For organizational activity to be aligned and stay aligned, plans and actions must be developed and agreed from WHY, to WHAT, to HOW.

To create and manage internal partnership, it works to develop and align on WHY (purpose), then WHAT (vision), then HOW (plan and actions). It does not work to try to align on HOW (plan and actions), then WHAT (vision), and then WHY (purpose). When internal partnership starts to break down and plans and actions (HOW) cannot be agreed, it works to mend the partnership by confirming alignment on WHY and WHAT first.

It does work to start with WHY

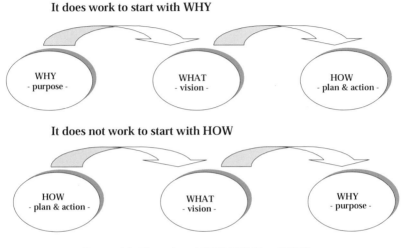

It does not work to start with HOW

Figure 4.3: The order of WHY, WHAT and HOW

We have identified that it works to have an organizational purpose that serves and is served by the purposes of the people within the organization.

Figure 4.4: Alignment of organizational and individual WHYs

Earlier we explained that high-performing organizations are high on vision (which constitutes the WHAT), and high on implementation (which constitutes the HOW). Bringing these ideas together, the high-performing organization has a purpose that is compelling for all of its stakeholders. This purpose will be realized by the vision of the organization and can be dependably implemented by its performance management system plan and actions (HOW). Purpose must come first, vision second and plan and actions last. WHAT and HOW exist inside of WHY; vision, plan and actions exist inside of purpose.

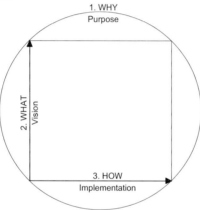

Figure 4.5: The relationship between Purpose, Vision and Implementation

Nice theory, but where do we apply it and how do we apply it? We will consider the following three examples, each of which builds on the other.

- Managing Paradigm to create effective interventions – managing by action
- Managing Paradigm to create a high performance team
- Managing Paradigm to implement a common performance management process

Managing Paradigm to create effective interventions

In the context of the Habits, the most immediate application is in creating an intervention – managing by action – creating corrective, preventive and breakthrough actions. The steps listed are worth understanding and applying when the going gets tough, when a problem seems insoluble and resistance, fears and fixed positions are coming into play.

Sometimes, as a manager of a difficult situation, the most powerful act of leadership is to request intervention or coaching from someone outside the situation. Culturally, requesting and accepting intervention by others when a situation is not being resolved, needs to be seen as a sign of strength, not of weakness.

Everyone knows that we sometimes need to 'think outside the box'. The problem is that we can see every box *except* the one that we are in. The following questions can be useful for creating an intervention by first getting 'outside the box'. They can be used as a framework for individual problem-solving, with or without a coach, or as a facilitated, team process.

There is magic in these questions because they enable us to see and name the box that we are in, which prevents us from creating a clear vision. They describe the box, step outside the box, and describe the vision for a future point in time. Even with a clear vision of WHAT is desired, we can get stuck on HOW it will be achieved. Without a process designed to create a breakthrough plan, we can only see options available in the PRESENT and see no way forward to create the FUTURE we envision.

The trick is to stand in the FUTURE and look back to the PRESENT – like a rock climber who makes the climb easier by first surveying the climb from above. She or he stands at the top of the rock face (in the FUTURE) and plans a route to make the climb from the bottom (the PRESENT) easy.

Exposing Paradigm (Drain the swamp)

Questions 1 and 2 can be used to expose beliefs that limit our solution-finding ability and also to expose the current Paradigm:

1. What is the situation requiring intervention (in the PRESENT)? Why did it happen?
2. Why may it be hard or impossible to resolve it? (Drain the swamp.)
3. What are the root causes?
4. If you suspect that the problem cannot be solved, suspend disbelief now and trust the process!

Articulating purpose (WHY)

5. WHY is it important, relevant, worth-it, to resolve the situation? What is the **purpose** of the intervention?

Clarifying a vision (WHAT)

6. WHAT is the desired situation at a specified time in the future? (The FUTURE.) Describe and visualize the desired FUTURE (not how it will be achieved, just what it will look like). The FUTURE is the desired outcome or the **vision** for the situation after the intervention.

Creating a plan from the FUTURE back to the PRESENT (HOW)

7. HOW did it look immediately before this situation was achieved. Repeat this step until the sequence of events from the desired FUTURE has been tracked back to the current situation (PRESENT).
8. Take this sequence of events, which starts in the future and works back to the present and arrange it in time, and adjust it until it is a credible plan.

Improvement

9. What can be learned?
10. How can it be applied? What actions will be taken to improve processes and plans to incorporate this learning?

Managing Paradigm to create a High Performance Team

The steps below provide a roadmap for creating and maintaining a cohesive, aligned, high performance team. They are not a formula for success and there are other road maps and less structured approaches that will work. The key point is to manage and maintain a Paradigm of partnership. This roadmap assumes that the project to be implemented is a win for the organization and that sponsorship, resources, and communications infrastructure are in place. However, the job of a High Performing Team is to create solutions, even when there are problems.

To create a high performing team:

- Create for yourself, as leader, a Paradigm of partnership – everyone is going to win

- With the proposed team, facilitate draining the swamp – capture and acknowledge issues and concerns

- Create buy-in for each member of the would-be team using the Buy-in Questions:
    - Is it credible?
    - Is it relevant?
    - Is it worth-it?
    - What actions will you take now?

The intended outcome is that each team member is committed to being on the team, so the first action is a decision to join the team, or engage with the other team members in creating a shared win.

Align as a team on what the project will do:

- WHY – the reason behind, the motivator for the project

- WHAT – the vision for the outcome of the project

- HOW – the plan for the project

- Implement the project, consciously managing and maintaining buy-in of the team and resolving issues from WHY to WHAT to HOW

The output of the above steps, a high performance team, is a group of people who have a shared vision and are committed to implementing it. The real outcome is in the results produced. If the team has the mission, for example, of 'implementing a common performance management process' across an organization, the outcome is a team committed to making this happen.

Managing Paradigm to implement a common performance management process

The *implementation* steps are identified later (in Chapter 10) as **Preparation**, **Pilot** and **Rollout**. The champion responsible for the Preparation and Pilot steps is recommended to pay continual attention to maintaining a High Performance Team as defined above.

Rollout of a successful pilot requires that people across multiple organization units buy-in. From a buy-in perspective, it can be useful to think in terms of two objectives, which in practice are achieved in parallel:

- Create a High Performance Team of people from across multiple organization units who will work as champions to create buy-in in their respective organization units.

- Support these champions to create a High Performance Team in each of their organization units to create buy-in within that organization unit.

Put in place management structures, practices and disciplines to encourage mutual support and learning among this group to help the individual champions to stay committed, even when the going gets tough.

Provide visible support in terms of acknowledgement, resources and technology.

These ideas are taken from workshop exercises that give hands-on experience with understanding Paradigm, creating buy-in, discovering purpose, creating vision and formulating breakthrough plans. All of these are tools for creating internal partnership. Internal partnership is a powerful tool in creating successful change.

Buy-in and the Balanced Scorecard

To create and maintain internal partnership the performance management structures of the organization must give satisfactory answers to the WHY, WHAT and HOW questions of every employee in the organization. The Balanced Scorecard can be a very effective tool for communicating strategy. A personalized Balanced Scorecard for each individual, team, department or even business unit, helps people to understand how the activities they perform and the results they personally produce, fit in with the overall value drivers, strategy and results of the organization.

Case Study: Personalized Balanced Scorecards at UltraViolet Design

When John returned to his office he enthusiastically arranged to meet his Administration and Search & Development teams to include them in developing the new Strategy, Objectives and Critical Success Factors. He was very interested to hear what his staff had to say about their operational measures.

After he had brought his staff up-to-date with progress so far and handed out copies of the Strategy, Objectives and Critical Success Factors, he asked, "What do you think of the work we have done so far and what do you think is next?"

"You've done a lot of work but I don't really see how you can quantify our jobs because reception doesn't have anything to do with the products we make, how we sell them or anything like that, " said Rosanna Grunvelt from the Reception team.

Inspired by Pete's easy facilitation, John smiled and pointed to the handout, "Let's review the Objectives and Critical Success Factors and see if there isn't one here which relates to your role."

Together the team reviewed the handout.

"I guess that I have something to do with customer satisfaction because I arrange the conference rooms for client meetings," Rosanna offered tentatively.

"Exactly," smiled John, *"are there any other areas where you see that you influence any of these Objectives?"*

Rosanna was growing more confident, *"Reception is the first place our customers see when they visit UVD, so we could have a lot to do with promoting an eco-friendly image. And,"* Rosanna paused to collect her thoughts, *"we are responsible for incoming and outgoing communications, so we have an effect on the money you make."*

"The Profit we make!" corrected John.

"Great," said John. *"Now, I think I need to give you all time to think about what we have been discussing today. Start to work out how you effect the UVD Objectives and what measures could help us manage our success and let's meet again tomorrow at the same time."*

The following day, John greeted everyone warmly. *"How have you been getting on with the Objectives since yesterday?"*

Rosanna's hand shot up and she started to speak, *"Well, I saw how completely stupid I have been about what I can do in my job."* She hurried on to explain herself, *"I didn't think that I had permission to change anything at UVD. I have been waiting for one of the Director's to tell me what to do rather than making suggestions. I also saw that there are a lot of things I could do to influence the Objectives and I think we need another Critical Success Factor in the area of the money..."* She corrected herself. *"The Profit we make."*

John's eyebrows raised in surprise, *"Really? What did you have in mind?"*

"The Critical Success Factors that you created with the managers have a lot to do with production and not a lot to do with the everyday running of the business. I think we need to create a Critical Success Factor for how the money we spend in every day

operations effects the profit. I could save money on our telephone system and out-going mail, for example," Rosanna replied.

"And Quality," shouted out Jim Simms from the Research & Development team. "We need to measure the quality of our materials and designs so we don't waste so much time fixing problems that could have been avoided."

"It sounds like you have all done a lot of thinking," complimented John. "Let's get all these ideas down so we can choose the best ones."

5. HABIT 3: KEEP IT SIMPLE

KEY POINTS

☑ Vision and strategy must be clearly articulated.

☑ To make sure that the strategy is delivered, the performance management process must be aligned with the strategy.

☑ Focus attention on a small number of Key Value Drivers (KVDs).

☑ Alignment is supported by using the same KVDs throughout the entire performance management process.

Less is more

"Truth is ever to be found in simplicity and not in the multiplicity of things."

Isaac Newton

It is right that this should be the shortest chapter in the book. After all, less is more! To focus on what is important, we must take focus away from what is not important. The less we have to think about, the more likely we are to keep track of it. That is why so many organizations identify and focus on the "Vital Few". The fewer strategies, the more likely they are to be implemented. The fewer critical success factors, the more likely they are to be considered critical. The fewer key performance indicators, the more likely they are to be 'key'. The fewer actions that are defined, the more likely they are to get done. However, for less to be more, the strategies, key value drivers, critical success factors and key performance indicators must be the right ones.

In many organizations, management reporting has developed over time without an overall vision or development plan. This sometimes results in reports and management information that are not really aligned with the activities, responsibilities and needs of the management team. This is especially when the management team was not involved in defining the reports. The reports may have been compiled by the Finance Department with budget tracking rather than performance improvement in mind. In addition, the role of the management team is not always clear. The role of the management team, at any level in the organization, is not just to meet and talk. It is to be a 'board of directors' that manages the organization's achievement of its strategy. The reports and management information must be designed to support the management team in delivering on their strategy. If the team is the Board of Directors of a large multinational or the Quality Team in a particular manufacturing plant, the context will be different, but the principle is the same.

Key Value Drivers (KVD) and the performance management process

The performance management process provides a powerful tool for aligning the organization. By linking strategy, budgeting/target setting, reporting and forecasting into an integrated process, an organization not only achieves excellence in each part of the process, but also aligns the information flows and activities in each part of the process. If every part of the performance management process refers to the same value drivers then the potential for confusion, misunderstanding and error is minimized. This consistency also supports the organization's need for simplicity and speed. The strategic plan of the corporate headquarters can still have a time-span measured in years, but the review of the plan can be done continually as needed. The strategic plan itself has become less complicated because it only focuses on the key items.

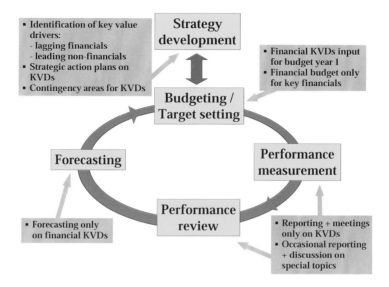

Figure 5.1: Linking the steps in the performance management process with key value drivers

The key concept is that a limited number of KVDs (Key Value Drivers) provide the link between stages in the performance management process. These KVDs which include lagging financial and leading non-financial value drivers are identified during the strategy development process as being the most important, critical items on which the organization has to focus to achieve success. The strategic action plans are centered around these key value drivers. The financial budget is made only for the limited number of key *financial* drivers. A complete, detailed budget for profit and loss and balance sheet is not needed. Hence, management only needs information about results and forecasts of future results in terms of these value drivers, and can therefore strictly focus on exceptional results (positive or negative). Contingency areas (which stipulate when higher management levels should consider intervening) only need to be established for these value drivers. (See Chapter 6 for a discussion of these contingency areas.)

An organization has to take care that the value drivers across the organization are aligned. Some of these KVDs will be the same for all parts of the organization. On a more detailed level, the critical success factors and key performance indicators will probably differ.

Beyond budgeting?

"Traditional budgeting sets not only a ceiling on costs but also a floor. It promotes centralization of decisions and responsibility, makes financial control an annual autumn event, absorbs significant resources across the organization, and acts as a barrier to customer responsiveness"

Bjartes Bognses, VP Corporate Control, Borealis

Currently, many organizations are looking to further simplify their performance management process by removing the budgeting step. Budgets were developed in the twenties to help organizations manage their assets and capital resource requirements. It took until the sixties before budgets started to be used for managing internal processes and for evaluating the performance of management. Today budgets are mainly used to set strategic and operational targets, to track the execution of the strategy and to control the organization's processes. However, there is growing concern with the budgeting process, both in the literature and within organizations. The main perceived problems with budgets are:

- Budgets can reinforce the command and control management model and thus undermine team working, delegation and empowerment.

- Because budgets are 'locked-in' once a year, they encourage 'inside the box' and incremental thinking. They tend to set a ceiling on growth expectations and a floor for cost reductions thus stifling real improvement breakthroughs. When the budget has been reached, there is no real incentive for managers to take advantage of possibilites for extra turnover or cost reductions.

- Budgets do not deal with most of the important drivers of shareholder value today. Strong brands, skilled people, excellent management processes, strong leadership, and loyal customers are assets that are outside the measurement orbit of the accounting system.

- Budgets may not provide the CEO with reliable current and forecast numbers. Budgets are typically extrapolations of existing trends with little attention being paid to anticipatory models. In addition, many organizations start developing the budget early in the year, thereby decreasing the relevance to the real situation of the organization in the new year.

- Budgets act as barriers to exploiting synergies across business units. Budgets encourage parochial behaviour, a 'defend your own turf' attitude, that is only reinforced by recognition and rewards linked to achieving the budgeted numbers.

- Budgets can be a bureaucratic, time-consuming exercise, and the time taken could be redeployed in more value creating activities. Budgets are often more detailed, containing more parameters than are actually needed. Budgets with this level of detail cost more time and effort than may be needed. In addition, in some organizations many iterations may take place between corporate and business unit management before consensus is reached on the budget level.

Why, then, given these disadvantages, do organizations still engage in the budgeting process? The answer lies in their long history of use in organizations and the resulting unchallenged position among the accepted management practices. There have been some attempts to streamline the process, like 'zero-base budgeting' and 'activity based budgeting', but these techniques often proved to be too difficult for large scale implementation. Other alternatives, like 'rolling forecasts', Balanced Scorecards, quarter-end combined with year-end prognoses, three-dimensional accounting, activity based costing/management and economic profit models all only solved part of the problem. Therefore, many organizations are now looking for an integrated solution, probably centered around rolling forecasting and measuring just the key value drivers. It will be very interesting to follow these developments in the next few years.

Figure 5.2: The future?

Case Study: Keeping Things Simple at UVD

John wrote all the team's ideas on the whiteboard. The sheer volume of ideas and measures staggered him.

During the break, John called Pete to give him an update.

"You won't believe the number of ideas and measures my team has come up with," John reported. "They just keep coming up with more and more. It is almost overwhelming."

"Don't I know it. People are amazing when they feel their contribution is being heard and accepted." replied Pete. "But don't forget to keep it simple. It is better to have just a few measures that

are successful than too many that are too difficult to manage and monitor."

John laughed. "I am glad you said that, I was starting to get really worried."

Returning to the conference room, John calmed the room after the break.

"We are now going to edit all these good ideas and measures into a handful of simple measures per department. That way we can make sure that what we decide to measure is easy to remember, track and monitor. No idea is a bad one, we just want to hone in on the key indicators."

A couple of weeks later, Pete called into the UVD office to check how things were working out. He stopped by at John's office and asked him if the ADBS system was working to the satisfaction of the UVD management team.

"We now use the system as the focus for all of our management meetings. I think that's what I expected. What I didn't expect was that all of the team would use it, too. Rosanna, on Reception, has taken on a personal mission to reduce costs. She's found a telephone supplier to cut costs by 28% based on our historic use. That saving is more than we pay her! Everyone seems to have got hold of the idea that there are a few key things we need to measure and that, if we get them right, all the rest will work."

Pete laughed, "Well done, people are full of surprises when you involve them. Have you noticed any changes in the way people work together outside the management team."

"Yes!" answered John. "They talk a lot more about WHY they are doing what they are doing. Almost every meeting centers on the measures in the Balanced Scorecard, even when I am nowhere near it. I almost feel guilty – they're doing my job!"

"Well done, John, that's called empowerment. Haven't you noticed that you are doing mine?" asked Pete.

6. HABIT 4: MANAGE BY EXCEPTION

KEY POINTS

☑ People suffer from information overload.

☑ Use exception reports like traffic light displays to show where attention is needed.

☑ Use exception reports to show performance against targets.

☑ Use exception reports to show every employee when service levels are being met and when bonuses are being achieved.

☑ Use contingencies in expected levels of Key Value Drivers (ranges around the targets) to give a clear framework for when intervention by measure owners and higher management levels is required.

An overload of information

Information overload is a common problem. The danger is that vital *information* is obscured by a mass of less important *data*.

We need to focus valuable management attention and time on the issues that really matter and take account of Habit 3: 'Keep it simple'.

Exception reporting gives managers the information they need to act upon.

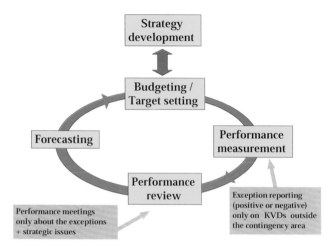

Figure 6.1: Exception-based reporting and review

Exception reporting for empowerment

An important drain on the effectiveness of managers is not lack of commitment, but lack of understanding of what is happening compared to what is needed. Exception reporting is a powerful tool for telling every team in the organization the score – how they are performing, compared to their targets. If employees are to be self-managing and self-motivating, it is necessary that they know the score. Exception reporting makes sure that the team does not waste a lot of time finding out the score, before making decisions and taking action.

When an incentive or bonus is related to the score, knowing the score can always be used to focus attention and enhance motivation. Organizations can significantly increase the return on investment from incentive and bonus payments by making sure that the team knows the score as they are playing the game. The purpose of the bonus payment is to motivate, focus and direct people. Good performance management information, including exception reports are an important tool for creating internal partnership.

A typical exception report shows an employee where they need to focus, for example by traffic lighting exceptions – showing missed targets in red and achieved targets in green. A Team Leader can look at the performance across their team in a single exception report. The exception report is used to celebrate the accomplishments of the high performers and to coach those who are falling behind.

So, at the level of every team, every team member, exception reports are important. What about in managing the whole organization?

Exception reporting in corporate performance management

Exception reports focus the attention of management on reporting performance that is outside a certain range (negative *or* positive) from the expected target. 'Traffic light' reporting is a way to quickly focus on these exceptions. Specific colors are used to express the percentage or actual value deviation from target. For example, the color red for more than 10% under target, yellow for 5 - 10% under target and green for on target (see Figure 6.2).

In corporate performance, the colors in the exception reports can also represent the management intervene areas defined in the budgeting process, where actual performance is outside the budget contingency area (see Figure 6.3). The red 'traffic light' could indicate that a corporate intervention is needed.

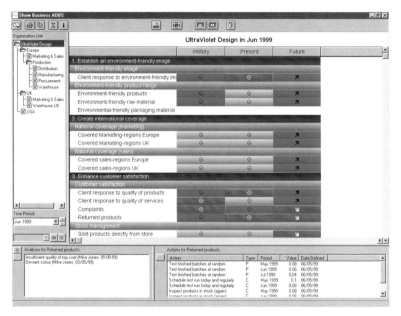

Figure 6.2: Example of a traffic light exception report

Typically, exceptions are defined with a number of color-coded levels. The exception condition is based on the relationship between the actual value, the budget, previous periods, etc.

Focus on exception meetings

In this example, we describe a model for exception reporting and management intervention from one of the best practice companies, a corporation with divisions and business units within divisions.

Organizations can use contingencies in the performance management process. Management can never guarantee that KVD levels will be achieved exactly as planned. Contingencies (① in Figure 6.3) can be defined which are performance ranges that represent acceptable deviations from the target. Only if business performance is outside the agreed contingency area will division management or corporate intervene and take on a more active (coaching) role. This active role includes more frequent performance reviews and more detailed reporting. In order to implement this type of 'management by exception', target KVD levels are agreed at the business level for a limited set of key financial performance indicators. Examples of such key indicators are Economic Value Added™, Net Operating Profit, Return on Capital Employed and Contribution Margin.

For each of the key indicators, contingencies are set between each division and corporate, as well as between each business and division. The contingencies are based on sensitivity analyses performed during the strategy development process. Management reports include traffic lights that show if actual or forecasted performances on the key financial indicators need divisional ('yellow' light) or corporate ('red' light) intervention (respectively ② and in ③ the figure), see also previous section. Performance reviews take place on an exception basis, as corporate or division management only intervene when *actual* or *forecasted* performance is outside the contingency areas.

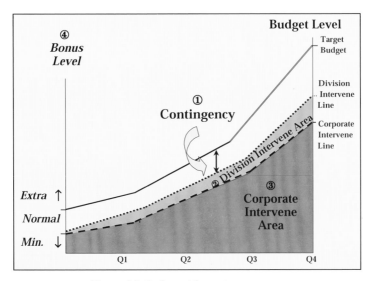

Figure 6.3: Budget with contingency areas

Finally, management compensation is dependent on year-end performance against KVD targets (④). For example, the more the actuals have fallen below the budget, the more the bonus is reduced. In the corporate intervene area no bonus is received at all. Outstanding performance above the agreed target results in an accelerated bonus.

The definition and use of contingency areas provides a clear structure for corporate and division management for the timing of interventions. It enables 'management by exception', thus allowing management sufficient time to focus on the real problem areas. When integrated with management reporting, contingencies can be translated to traffic lights, thereby supporting management's focus. Finally, contingency areas allow for reasonable deviations from KVD target levels, based on a sensitivity or risk analysis.

The level of detail of the budget impacts the concept of contingencies. Setting contingencies for every budget line item is time-consuming and will be unmanageable. Consequently, a limited set of KVDs is used as the focus for exception reporting.

Case Study: Exception reporting at UltraViolet Design

At the next management meeting, Pete introduced performance management by exception.

"You can all see the increased employee participation at UVD as a result of the work we have done so far."

"Yes, but have you seen how much time they spend chatting about the stuff. Before, I told them what to worry about, now they spend time trying to do all the filtering that I've spent years learning to do in an instant." suggested Gary.

"No benefits, then?" asked Pete, putting his head to one side.

"Well, yes, they work harder, make less mistakes and complain less!" smiled Gary. Everybody laughed - especially Gary.

"I rest Pete's case!" answered John.

"And I'd like to take up Gary's case!" responded Pete. "Gary, how do you do that thing you do?" Everyone laughed again as Gary looked at Pete suspiciously. "How do you manage to do all that filtering in an instant?"

"Oh!" responded Gary, with relief. "I compare the key figures with what I expect and track down the ones which are out of line."

"Management by Exception – a Habit of high performance. Next we'll build management by exception into your performance management system. That way anyone can see how different KPIs compare with targets. Your team will be able to see the exceptions instantly – with bad numbers in red and good numbers in green!"

"So, what's my job?" asked Gary.

"What do you do once you've found the exceptions?" asked Pete.

"Do something about fixing them!" replied Gary.

Pete nodded. "OK, there are still Corrective Actions to take, so you're not out of a job. Now, let's focus on how to support management by exception."

They spent the rest of the meeting looking at how the same principle could be applied to monitoring and acting on different Key Performance Indicators.

John could see that managing by exception could be a powerful tool for him as CEO, so he brought the subject up at his next one-on-one meeting with John. By now, John really enjoyed these meetings with Pete. John was right, Pete had some useful input.

" First of all, target values must be determined for each of the Key Performance Indicators you invented," Pete explained. "The target values need not necessarily be 100% accurate right from the start. When you select a value which is really too far off the mark, you will notice this soon enough and then you can adjust the value, preferably after first having consulted the others," Pete assured him.

*"Once the target has been set, give the staff a chance to fulfill it. I'm not saying don't get involved, that would be crazy. No, become involved when the actual performance differs from the target and then **ask** the key performance indicator owner if they need help or review the indicator."*

"Oh, I see," John interrupted. "If performance isn't on track then I can make suggestions and help achieve the target rather than just take over."

"Exactly," replied Pete. "Don't fall into the rut that many managers do, when it isn't working you don't have to take control."

John blushed.

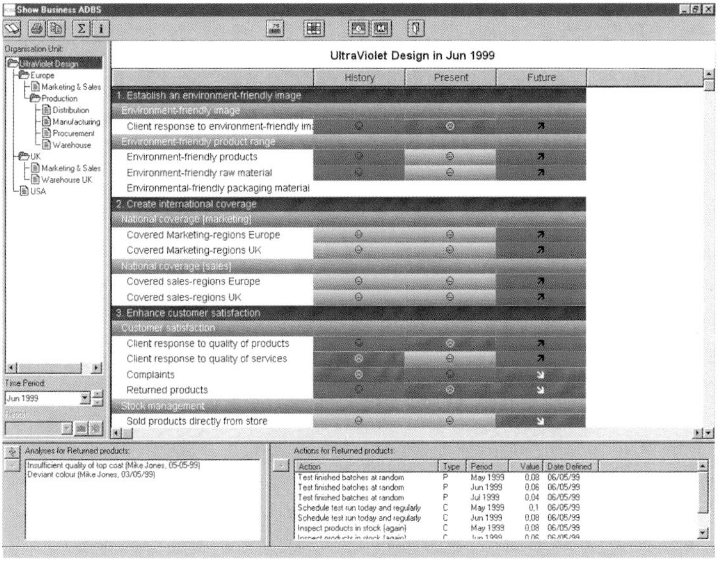

Figure 6.4: KPI Monitor - monitors fulfillment of UVD strategy

Helen met Pete to find out if there was any way she could use ADBS more efficiently to free up some time to deal with the other issues she was facing.

She asked, "Pete, I am under a lot of time pressure at the moment because of the different developments in the organization. How do you suggest that I use exception reporting to find where I need to be focussing my attention? Is it the UK? Is it Americas? Is it the home market?   Normally, I have to filter a whole lot of information before I know what needs attention."

"Well", replied Pete, "In principle, we need to figure out what filtering you do and build that into the traffic lighting of the ADBS."

Helen was looking frustrated.

"What's bothering you?" asked Pete.

"Oh, nothing, I'm just stressed." replied Helen.

*Pete smiled and explained. "That's not what I meant! What is the **business problem** that's bothering you?"*

"Oh, I see." exclaimed Helen, "I know that I need to track down some financial issues with product returns and I don't have the time. I can't find anyone in production, so it's pretty irritating. I need to know where the 'returns' problem is showing up because it has some pretty heavy financial consequences. That's the top of the list, but there are about 10 others before I pick my daughter up tonight!" answered Helen.

"OK. That's what I needed." said Pete. "Take a look at the ADBS. Let's take product returns as an example. The Strategic Objective of 'delivering high-quality products' has the Critical Success Factor 'high-quality product range'. This is measured with the KPI 'percentage of returned products' which - you're right - is high. That's why it's red!"

"OK, I can see that," said Helen, "but I need to know how the red breaks down, what the number is and what we're doing about it."

Pete talked as Helen moved the mouse. He showed her how to compare returned products across markets and how to drill-down to Corrective Actions. Helen now had all her answers.

Pete looked puzzled and asked, "Just one question. Weren't you shown how to do that in the training?"

Helen hid her face as if to apologise. "I missed the course! I was fighting fires... like the one that you just put out for me!"

They both smiled.

"I'll book myself on the course," continued Helen.

"Great!" answered Pete.

7. HABIT 5: MANAGE BY ACTION

KEY POINTS

☑ Actions are important, but they are often not reported, tracked or managed.

☑ Performance measurement is passive. Active performance management is needed: taking swift corrective action to deal with issues as soon as they are identified.

☑ Replace past-based measurement, fault and blame, with forward-looking measurements, root cause analysis and corrective action.

☑ Make managers visibly accountable for the execution of actions, and track the results of these actions.

☑ Preventative actions correct forecasted problems before they impact. Breakthrough actions achieve breakthrough results created by 'out of the box' thinking.

Measuring is interesting, action makes the difference

"Action is eloquence."
William Shakespeare

"The objective is not simply to take action, but to take meaningful action."
Kröger et.al.
Spearheading Growth

To measure performance outputs just for the sake of measurement does not add value. The difference is made when management does something about, and with, the measured outputs. Do managers analyse and understand results and do they turn their insights into actions? Research shows that in many organizations the vital action step is not formalized and actions are not tracked.

Management reports mainly report on outputs. They do not keep track of the actions that cause results. Often, managers are not made accountable for defining and taking action. As a consequence, no one monitors actions. And when managers do not take any corrective action, there is no record of this inactivity. The only evidence of the lack of action is that problems persist.

The way managers and organizations deal with bad results is a major determinant of their success. The recipe for failure is to monitor only past based measures, like revenue and profit, and when targets are missed, decide who's fault it is and blame or even fire them. Blame as a response to performance failures promotes fear in the culture. Fear stifles the ability of managers to think creatively, to re-connect with vision and strategy, and to find solutions to difficult problems. The recipe for success is to include forward looking measures, like customer satisfaction, process quality and development of human skills, analyse the results for learning opportunities, and create corrective actions to put the organization back on track. The role of a coach is to help the person they are coaching to believe that the problem is solvable and that they are able to solve it and to focus attention away from fault and blame and towards understanding, corrective action and learning.

Recipe for failure: performance gets worse

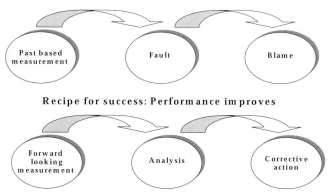

Figure 7.1: Recipes for failure and success

Identifying corrective actions requires creative, lateral thinking. Delivering on corrective actions requires focus, accountability and monitoring. Managing actions, as well as monitoring results, is a powerful way to shift towards a culture of responding, learning and continuous improvement.

In some cultures focus has been on meeting budgets, rather than on making the business successful. Figures relating to outcomes are threatening as they provide transparency of value creation, thereby destroying 'little kingdoms', which have focused on input and output, rather than outcome. In these 'stuffy' organizations a performance management system which provides transparency of results and actions is a 'breath of fresh air'. If the outcomes and value creation that are measured, managed and improved relate to strategy, then performance of the organization is likely to follow.

Apply corrective and preventative action planning

To make most effective use of management reporting, an organization needs a culture of openness, transparency and self-improvement. This culture has to be supported by reports and systems that contain future-oriented information, because this stimulates pro-active and anticipative behaviour. These reports and systems should also be used to monitor actions (including agreements, people accountable, expected results, and actual results).

More and more organizations are including action reports in their management reporting set. These action reports describe the corrective actions that are implemented when the actual results do not meet the targets. Preventative action reporting reports on how forecast problems are being addressed. If the forecasted result for the next period and the target for that same period deviate outside a predefined range, preventative actions are formulated to make sure that the target will be achieved after all. Included in the action plan are the projected results of the preventative actions over time, as effects of the actions may not be visible immediately and can have impact on the results of coming periods.

Figure 7.2 illustrates a preventative action report for one key value driver. It displays an unfavourable deviation between forecast and target, the underlying root cause analysis, the description of preventative actions and the expected results for the value driver in the coming periods.

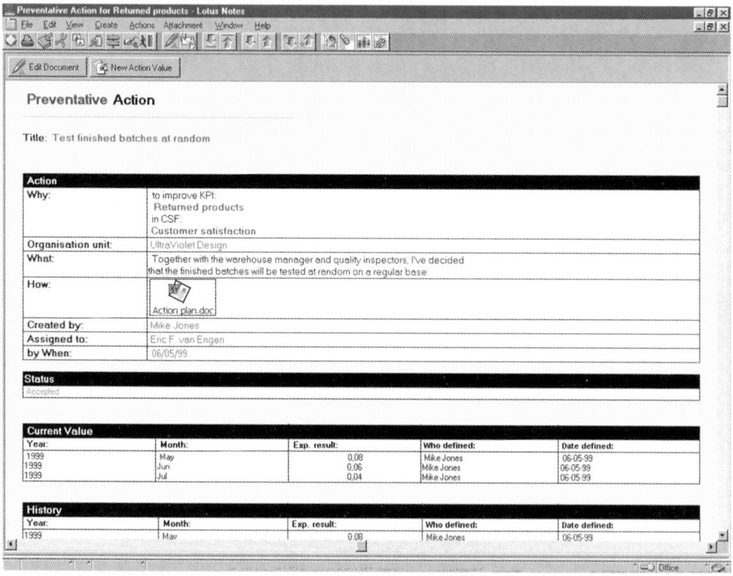

Figure 7.2: Preventative action with forecast impact

Breakthrough actions aim to produce results 'outside the box'.

Defining corrective, preventative and breakthrough actions

> *[Faced with a problem] "At one extreme, we can allow ourselves to be overwhelmed. At the other, we can simply go on a picnic or take a holiday and ignore it. The third possibility is to face up to the*

situation directly. This involves examining it, analysing it, determining its causes and finding out how to deal with them."
His Holiness the Dalai Lama

Sounds like TQM (Total Quality Management)! Often when corrective action is required to correct a measure of performance, the owner of that measure has not corrected it because there is no obvious solution. The challenge is to question assumptions and think outside the box. It is natural to feel defensive when there is a possibility of intervention by peers or upper management. The challenge for the person making the intervention is to get the problem solved and to leave the manager more able to solve future problems. To do this, it is essential to have a Paradigm of partnership for the coaching relationship. A good place for the coach to start is by affirming their respect for the manager, their intention to help, not to judge, by acknowledging any circumstances which make the situation hard for the managers and providing any praise of the managers which is due.

One risk of intervention in the activities of a manager is that it can leave the manager feeling disrespected and disempowered. A successful intervention helps the manager to identify the box in which they are thinking and to identify a solution that they can believe in. The job of the coach is to believe that the problem has a solution and to believe in the ability of the manager to solve the problem. The challenge for higher management in providing coaching is to intervene, without disempowering the person they are meant to be coaching. Ideally the manager should be left with more understanding of the current situation (PRESENT), a clearer vision of the desired situation (FUTURE) and a plan to get from the PRESENT to the FUTURE which they can believe in and deliver on. (See a recommended process for creating this plan in Habit 2).

The word 'breakthrough' signifies breaking through boundaries, assumptions and limiting beliefs. Breakthrough Actions are only possible after a shift of Paradigm (see Habit 2). The mechanics of recording and implementing a breakthrough action are much the same as the mechanics of recording a corrective or preventative action

In most organizations, every business unit, department, team and individual manager has more to-dos than they can accomplish. Just as we define strategy, budgets, reports and forecasts based on key value drivers, it is essential to focus on the Vital Few Actions, which make the most contribution for the least effort. Actions are best prioritized by looking for the 'low hanging fruit': if it is **easy** and it makes a **big difference**, then do it first. For example, if you have a list of suggested actions to improve a KPI, list the actions in one column, with the impact (from 1 to 5) in a second column and the cost (1 to 5) in a third column. In a fourth column, calculate Impact divided by Cost. The highest scoring actions are the low hanging fruit.

"The great end of life is not knowledge but action."
Thomas Henry Huxley

Case Study: Action reporting at UltraViolet Design

Helen was reviewing traffic light reports. She felt there was something missing. The report assumed target values, actual values and deviations. It also showed that, until now, some countries had managed to realize the targets, whereas others required extra attention. The percentage of returned products, for instance, turned out to be higher than the target value across all the countries. Helen wondered what Corrective Actions Mike Jones, Head of Manufacturing, was planning to stop the increase and deliver the target.

She called Mike who was very enthusiastic on the telephone.

Mike was excited about the Traffic Light report he was exploring in ADBS. He said, "I was alarmed when I saw the problem with returns but I'm on the case!"

Helen asked, "Good, what do you have in mind?"

"Well, I haven't really decided what to do yet. In fact, at the moment, it could go either way. Better or worse," he clarified. He

knew that this was not what Helen wanted to hear but it was the truth.
"I'll work on it, Helen. It's my highest priority."
  "Thanks, Mike." said Helen.
  The call ended.

  *Helen felt very uncomfortable after the telephone conversation
with Mike. At least now she understood what was missing. She
needed an insight into the future – projections and what was being
done to impact the future – and that is 'actions'. Pete had talked
about adding Corrective Actions to their reporting. Now seemed like
a good time!*

  *A week had gone by since Helen Case talked to Mike Jones
about the high percentage of returned products. In the meantime, she
had contacted Pete Fields and made an appointment to talk things
through. The day after the Quarter 1 figures had been released
Helen, Pete and Mike met. They decided to focus on the percentage
of returned products.*
  *Helen asked Mike what his forecast was for the following
period.*
  *Mike had been working on it. He explained the complexity.
UltraViolet Design produced for stock, which meant that they
delivered part of the April sales from stock. Besides that, not all
clocks in the stores had been sold yet. Hence, Mike did not really
expect a decrease in the number of returned products. In fact, he
thought it would still average around 15%. He had to initiate some
action to improve the percentage of returned products.*
  *Mike explained his thorough analysis - identifying the cause of
the high percentage of returned products. It turned out that most of
the returned products had a deviant colour: they looked tarnished
and faded. After having consulted the manufacturing foremen, Mike
thought it likely that the protective layer sealing the topcoat was not
up to quality. This had happened before. Today they were going to
perform a test run to see whether this was the real cause.*
  *It also turned out that UltraViolet Design's quality control was
not testing products as comprehensively as they could. It was*

possible that the clocks left the production line in good condition and that the colour change emerged after a certain period of time. The test run was expected to give a conclusive answer to this possibility. Fortunately, the next production run of clocks was not scheduled until the end of next week. Thus, there was no immediate need to adjust the production planning. (By this time, Helen was getting lost in detail).

"So Mike, what is the bottom line? What are we doing about it?" Helen asked.

Mike listed his intended actions:

- *The test run has been scheduled and will take place today.*

- *The products in stock will be inspected again and the products with color defects will be taken out of stock.*

- *The finished batches will be tested again, at random. This will be done on a regular basis so as to reduce product quality problems in future.*

Mike looked at them both with pride. "I expect that these steps will bring the actual value to the target level within three months."

Helen and Pete were not used to this kind of detail but they thought they understood the actions.

"Mike," asked Helen, "have you considered the cost of the actions so that we can choose to carry out only cost-effective actions."

Mike answered that the "bottom-line" cost was two man-days. He expanded, "Tests are run on a regular basis. For the first action all we are doing is bringing forward next week's test. Testing the products in stock will cost us a person day. The additional testing will cost a further day. That's two days in total. "

Helen and Pete were impressed. Together they created a future and action oriented report for April 1999 in ADBS. Now the WHY, WHAT and HOW of the Corrective Action would be documented.

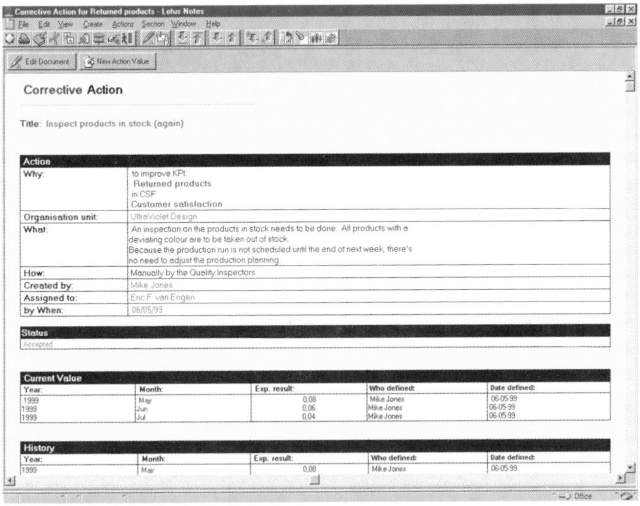

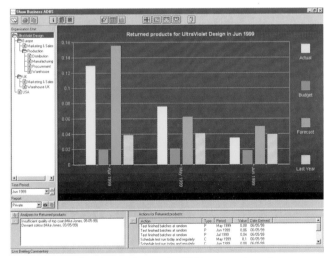

Figure 7.3: Corrective action to reduce product returns

Figure 7.4: Action Report for UVD returned products.

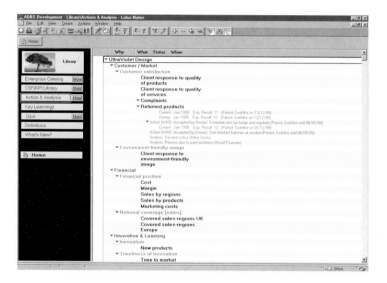

Figure 7.5: A record of Actions and the Strategy, CSF and KPI to which they relate.

Suddenly everyone was talking about Corrective Actions and Root Causes, and saying "If it is broke, fix it."

The chatter among the team at UVD was that John had turned over a new leaf. He must have had some kind of awakening because he was asking about solutions, rather than look for someone to blame. No one knew why but everyone suspected Pete.

8. HABIT 6: CREATE INFORMATION TRANSPARENCY

KEY POINTS

☑ Everyone needs information and knowledge to support high performance.

☑ Information transparency gives people what they need but only what they have a right to.

☑ 90% of the business value can be provided with a Performance Management Portal containing KPI reports or a Balanced Scorecard, actions and a catalog of other performance management knowledge assets.

☑ A Performance Management Portal uses 'middleware' to deliver information from multiple sources to distributed users.

☑ Empowerment requires a shift of focus from delivering performance management information to a few people to delivering simpler information to many people.

☑ Information transparency grows organically, it cannot be created with a 'Big Bang'.

☑ Enterprise Resource Planning (ERP) systems are used to 'do business'. Adding a Performance Management Portal is the next logical step to help to manage the business.

☑ The Performance Management Portal replaces printout and emailed requests with self-service shared information.

☑ To succeed, information transparency requires ground rules to build trust and support openness.

The need for information transparency

"However long we may drag our feet, we will be forced to accept that information – freely generated and freely exchanged – is our only hope for organization. If we fail to recognize its generative properties, we will be unable to manage in this new world."

Margaret J. Wheatley
'Leadership and the New Science'

In many organizations managers have become so used to waiting for changes to their management information that they have given up asking for them. Highly skilled analysts are effectively acting as information 'gophers' responding to particular requests, fire-fighting problems with no time to create better, automated information supply. Even standard, regular reports are often held up due to lack of automation and physical handling delays. Because security issues with email and intranet publishing limit what can be done safely and at acceptable cost, reports are often delivered to only a sub-set of the people who could benefit from them. Business users of information become dissatisfied with IT or analyst professionals who seem unresponsive. IT professionals see their customers as demanding and unrealistic.

To support high performance, the requirement is simple: *information transparency*. Every person in the organization must have easy access to the information that they may need to do their job. With effective transparency, the information is only limited to the reports that they have the security rights to see and use. Information transparency replaces slow, inefficient, frustrating interchanges between creators and users of reports with self-service delivery. The result of information transparency is improved decision making, increased productivity and better relationships between suppliers and users of management information.

Information transparency requires easy access to information from many sources. To be practical for a large organization, information transparency must be achieved at low cost per additional business user. One solution would be to provide access to many different tools over an intranet, but this means that users must learn many different interfaces and that many different tools must be maintained and supported. Ease of use requires an easy to use, fast, simple, common user interface. The needs of information transparency define the requirements for a **Performance Management Portal**, which provides a common interface to information from many sources and supports the performance management process.

Before looking at systems architectures, let us consider the business need. One problem in finding out what people need from information systems is that they are often resigned and accepting of what they get. It is easy to criticise what is provided, but hard to consider what is really needed.

Part of our investigation has been to systematically analyze the information needs in a number of organizations across many communities of potential users of management information in an organization. This shows that in every organization there is a spectrum of needs for business intelligence and performance management information. These needs range from the need of a few analysts to use sophisticated data mining tools to the pervasive need of every business person for very simple performance management information.

The most striking conclusion is that the delivery of simple performance management information accounts for 80% to 90% of the business value which can be added through a performance management system. In most organizations, delivering 90% of the business value requires 10% of the functionality and complexity and a relatively small proportion of the cost. The first objective of a Performance Management Portal is to fulfill this need.

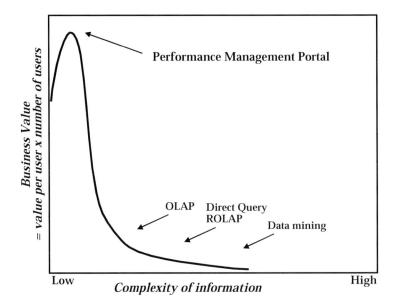

Figure 8.1: The 90% - 10% rule of business value

Across many organizations, in diverse industry sectors, there are common themes that further define the requirements for a Performance Management Portal:

- Almost everyone would benefit from some amount of management information.

- The potential needs of many people are ignored, typically for reasons of cost of ownership relating to systems and software cost, support cost and maintenance cost. The cost of ownership is simply too high.

- The majority of information needs (80 to 90% of individual queries and requests) are very simple and fall into two categories which can be fulfilled by a Performance Management Portal which provides:

- performance management information to show performance indicator results against service levels;
- enterprise reporting providing access to a library of documents and reports, providing the information which a person *may* need to support effective performance management, but only what they have a security right to receive.

- There typically exists a range of information needs in a company. This range of needs includes: the mass requirement for simple information; a smaller number of users requiring simple business analysis tools (Desktop OLAP); a smaller number requiring OLAP (slice and dice On-line Analytical Processing) tools; and, finally, an even smaller number of highly-specialized analysts requiring specialist tools, for example for data mining.

- There is normally a backlog of requirements for management information and reports leaving analysts stressed and overworked.

- Analysts typically spend between thirty to seventy percent of their time as information 'gophers' preparing and distributing reports.

- The solution of providing complex query tools to every user is costly and normally fails if the software requires more than minutes of end-user training.

- The most effective solution to solving the requirement for the mass delivery of reports is to automate repeated reports, and to deliver them through an easy to manage electronic catalog.

- The value derived from reporting, OLAP and data mining tools can be dramatically increased by effectively cataloging and publishing the reports they produce.

- Most organizations have a data warehouse and reporting strategy. Adding a Performance Management Portal to data warehouse projects can dramatically improve the return on investment achieved without a proportionate increase in cost.

To summarize the business requirement, the information transparency required to support performance management has two aspects:

- Performance management information which tracks KPI progress and gives people the information they need to know whether the organization and their accountabilities are on track. At a strategic level, this can be delivered by implementing a top down performance management system (like a Balanced Scorecard). It must be scaleable over time otherwise it can create more problems than it solves when people below a certain level in the organization have no access to performance information. (In addition to strategic measurement, using the Balanced Scorecard, most large organizations have tens or hundreds of initiatives that require tracking and monitoring of operational KPIs, for example measuring quality, service level reports, etc. The portal should provide for both strategic and operational performance management.)

- Enterprise reporting which is a 'catch-all' for all of the other reports and documents which people may need to participate in the performance management process. It provides transparency of reports, but only shows people the ones which they have a security right to see. This need can be fulfilled by implementing a one-stop-shop catalog to contain reports and management information from many systems in a single repository.

In addition, most large organizations have tens or hundreds of initiatives that require tracking and monitoring (for example, measuring quality, service level reports, etc).

Creating the Performance Management Portal

Many organizations have a strong foundation for performance management, with an existing architecture of layered information systems:

- an Executive or Management Information Systems (EIS/MIS)
- fed from OLAP databases – to allow slicing and dicing of summary information
- fed from a data warehouse – providing a single store of data and a single consistent 'version of the truth' about different aspects of the business, with data drawn from different sources
- fed from operational systems data, including, for example, ERP data.

Each of these toolsets and layers has value. Each supports or provides some part of the total management information and reporting requirement of the organization. ERP vendors are recognizing that they can add significant value for their customers by extending the ERP system from automating the operation of the business, to supporting excellent performance management. Providing a data warehouse or OLAP database capability is one step, but the warehouse in itself does not support performance management, so ERP vendors are enabling performance management as the next value-adding step for their customers. Early indicators suggest that this extension of, or evolution of, the ERP system will be a dramatic contributor to organizational effectiveness allowing established organizations to achieve the leapfrog in speed and responsiveness which they need to thrive in the New Economy.

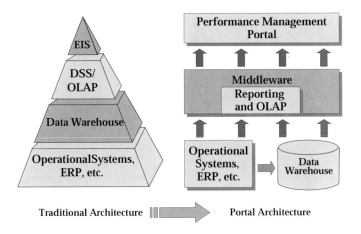

Figure 8.2: Using Middleware to deliver a Performance Management Portal

The traditional architecture for performance measurement has a number of limitations in relation to effectively supporting a world class performance management process:

- there is not necessarily any relationship between the information supplied and the strategy and goals which it should support (see Habit 1: Deliver on the strategy and goals);

- the cost of delivering secure focused information to every employee, to support effective management and decision making is often too high to be economical, so only a subset of people have the information they need to be fully empowered (see Habit 2: Create and manage internal partnership, and Habit 6: Information transparency);

- there is potentially an information overload (see Habit 3: Keep it simple, and Habit 4: Manage by exception);

- there is no support for action management (see Habit 5: Manage by action);

- often much resource has gone into developing the middle two layers (data warehouse + DSS/OLAP), which from a management information point-of-view is not necessarily sufficient because (see Figure 8.2) there is no support for the needs of the majority of business users.

To summarize, the traditional systems architecture can only partially support the Habits of high-performing organizations. Can we improve on this architecture to provide information transparency for performance management, cost effectively, across an organization? The following approach is one way to satisfy the business need:

- Information and reports are related to the strategy, by specifying, the critical success factors and key performance indicators that they support (support of Habit 1: Deliver on the strategy and goals).

- Cost-of-ownership can be dramatically reduced by using intranet and groupware tools. These provide the functionality required for secure transparency with low cost of ownership by providing a foundation for an open, secure, scaleable portal for performance management (support of Habit 2: Create and manage internal partnership, and Habit 6: Information transparency).

- Information is filtered, traffic-lighted and selected to provide and highlight only that which is strategically and personally relevant (support of Habit 3: Keep it simple, and Habit 4: Manage by exception).

- There is simple workflow support for action management (support of Habit 5: Manage by action).

- Existing information sources and reporting tools are leveraged by using a Performance Management Portal to provide management information for a large number of users (support of Habit 7: Leverage technology).

Managing in the New Economy requires that people across the organization are empowered to make good decisions, fast. This contrasts with the needs of a directive management style where a small number of people make decisions for the entire organization and everyone else 'does their job'. To support empowerment, the focus of management reporting is shifting:

- from providing complex information to a small number of decision-makers
- to also providing simple performance management information to empower many more people in making good decsions and creating business value.

The business value created for the organization is the sum of the business value created by each person.

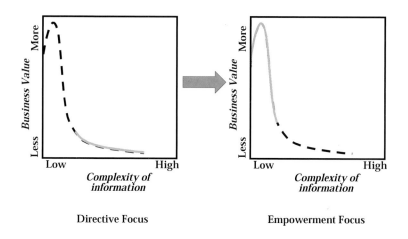

Directive Focus

Empowerment Focus

Figure 8.3: The new focus is on increased business value by empowering people throughout the organization with less complex information

When an ERP system is in place (or planned) the performance management system can improve the organization's ability to continuously improve and leverage much of the investment in ERP. This is because:

- Process descriptions, made while implementing the ERP system, can be used as the basis for designing key performance indicators.

- Reporting can now take place on processes that have been redesigned based on the organization's strategy.

- The consistent, accurate data in the ERP system can be consolidated directly for calculation of metrics in performance management.

When taking a Performance Management Portal approach, it is best to use the same portal framework (with different content) for different organization units. Even though different organization units may use different operational and ERP systems, the Performance Management Portal provides a standard template for information transparency. Taking the portal approach gives every organization unit the ability to manage and organise its own information and knowledge and to control who can see it. It is an effective way to create standardization across a large organization, without having to standardize every operational system, ERP system, data warehouse and reporting tool. This effectively refits the organization for working effectively in the New Economy, without requiring a massive investment in replacing existing systems, (which work as they are), with new organization-wide standards.

To re-cap, the performance management portal should provide every user in the organization, wherever they are, with access to:

- information to support the performance management process, including the Balanced Scorecard;

- actions and action tracking;

- information and reports which they may need from all of the key business intelligence tools, data warehouses and data-marts in use in the organization;

- links to data warehouse query and business intelligence tools, subject to security, to allow use of the tools themselves;

- unstructured information like strategic plans and presentations;

- qualitative information like analysis and commentary on information.

A checklist and the suggested criteria for the development or selection of a performance management portal are provided in Appendix C and D respectively.

The role of data warehouses and data-marts

Our focus here is on enabling high-performing organizations through information transparency. Transparency requires quick, easy, intuitive access to information. The source data for this information may be structured or unstructured data. A data warehouse approach is suitable for highly structured data, but not for the qualitative information like the commentary and shared insights that combine with quantitative information to make knowledge. A complete approach to information transparency must facilitate transparency of data warehouse information, as well as other kinds of knowledge (for example, action status and workflow, strategic plans, competitive reports, policies and mission, strategy and values).

For the structured data, one approach is to create a central data warehouse for use by all parts of a large organization. Another approach is to implement smaller warehouses and data-marts in business units. If data for the entire organization is stored in a single database, it is referred to as a 'data warehouse'. If data is stored for one specific department, a specific business process or a specific analytical purpose, the term data mart is often used. Normally a combination of the two will be the ideal solution. The balance chosen by a particular organization unit will depend on history (where the data is today), culture (centralized or not) and, of course, the immediate needs of the business to have information which may not be available in the corporate warehouse. As a result, any comprehensive approach to information transparency must facilitate transparent use of information from a central data warehouse as well as from distributed data-marts. A spectrum of business intelligence tools allows data from the warehouse to be viewed and analyzed for different purposes.

Data from data warehouses and data-marts can be used to: calculate KPIs that feed into the performance management system; generate reports for cataloging and delivery; perform analyses in OLAP tools; answer ad-hoc questions from end users or analysts; and support 'data mining', in which large quantities of data are analysed algorithmically in order to detect relationships and make predictions.

In recent years, software and hardware prices for data storage and analysis have steadily dropped, facilitating new levels of technology-supported customer knowledge, one-to-one marketing using data mining and segmentation for data discovery. The same systems permit new levels of reporting and analysis to support better understanding of the business and the marketplace and better informed strategy formulation. These are all aspects of business intelligence. By combining internal data (such as sales and invoice data) and external data (such as consumer data), new insights are possible and new business opportunities can be created. The information transparency provided by a Performance Management Portal can bring the benefits of the data warehouse and reporting tools to everyone in a large organization, by making the key outputs easily and securely available.

Ground rules for information transparency

Information transparency allows information to move up the organization and down the organization. With a Paradigm of internal partnership in place (see Habit 2), information transparency can help every business to achieve high performance by: communicating strategy throughout the organization; deploying strategy down the organization; focussing and managing action throughout the organization; and helping to create a partnership between management and employees at all levels.

However, there are pitfalls. Efficient knowledge sharing and learning requires **transparency**. Transparency requires **openness**. Openness requires **trust**. Trust requires **ground rules**. Information transparency can fail to deliver the benefits if there are not clear ground rules that deal with the potential pitfalls. It is important that we do not lose the opportunity of excellence in performance management, because we did not create appropriate ground rules. The following ground rules can work as a starting point:

- The critical success factors, key performance indicators and/or Balanced Scorecard are owned where strategy is created: at the business level.

- The business level chooses what information can be seen from higher levels in the organization. This is, by default, only what is already publicly available.

- Key performance indicator information and related actions will not be used against a manger, only to support that manager.

- The business level management chooses what information to share with which employees.

- Key performance indicators and the Balanced Scorecard are used by top management as a tool for support and coaching, rather than as a tool for identifying fault and apportioning blame.

With these ground rules, the Performance Management Portal can remove labour and cost from every business unit. Without them, business units may resist implementation of the portal, not because it is a bad thing for the business, but because they fear loss of control and independence.

Case Study: Information Transparency at UVD

Today, everyone in UVD can see how the organization is doing. The Strategy, CSFs and KPIs were relatively easy to find and publish - but no Actions are published. Somehow people didn't take to the idea of making their Corrective Actions public.

Information transparency was greeted with some suspicion at first. People chose not to make Corrective Actions public. The tide turned when John realized that a new culture of openness was needed to enable information transparency.

"Pete, why is it that no one seems to want to put in their Corrective Actions into the system?" John asked in exasperation.

Typically, Pete answered with a question. "Why do you think? Is there any risk for them? See if you can find out by asking."

A few days later, they resumed the conversation.
"So," asked Pete, "what did you find out?"
"They thought I'd beat them over the head with it if they didn't produce the result."
"Did you ever do that?" asked Pete.
"Yes. But not any more." replied John.
"If you shows that you can be trusted not to use information against the people who provide it, you'll get your transparency of Actions."

9. HABIT 7: LEVERAGE TECHNOLOGY

KEY POINTS

☑ Leverage existing business intelligence tools and IT infrastructure - don't just replace them.

☑ A performance management portal leverages a combination of technologies to support best practice.

☑ Best practice performance management requires enterprise support for communication (Email), collaboration (gathering and sharing of reports, knowledge and learning) and co-ordination (collaboration in time and process for action management and continuous improvement).

☑ Replication is required to provide a virtual portal, so that different people on different networks and stand-alone laptop computers can work together with the same data as a high performance team.

☑ Highest level security is required, with flexible control, based on position in organization, role, management level, etc.

☑ To deliver these essentials at low cost of ownership requires the full power of groupware or an intranet.

Leverage the IT infrastructure, don't replace it

In the New Economy, organizations must use information technology to enable world-class performance. In discussing the preceding Habits, we have identified key business needs, which in turn create requirements on technology. Leveraging technology means delivering these Habits using the technology available or expected, in the most effective and cost effective manner.

In the preceding chapters, we have discovered that performance management is a process, which involves targeting, measuring exceptions, taking action and learning. In addition to the ability to present a Balanced Scorecard, chart and tabulate data and traffic light exceptions, we discussed that a Performance Management Portal requires:

- **Communication** - the notification of people when information changes.

- **Collaboration** - sharing a combination of quantitative data like specific key performance indicators, qualitative information like strategic plans, textual analysis and actions. Collaboration, by co-creating and sharing rich information, is the foundation for knowledge management.

- **Co-ordination** - people work together on fulfilling requests and taking actions. Co-ordination is the foundation for efficient, collaborative-working business processes.

The combination of Communication, Collaboration and Co-ordination defines groupware as *the* information technology foundation for best practice performance management and hence organizational effectiveness.

Use of groupware and intranet for fast and efficient distribution

Today's groupware and intranet technology mean that information transparency, with workflow for corrective actions and continual improvement, can now be delivered at an enterprise scale with low cost of ownership.

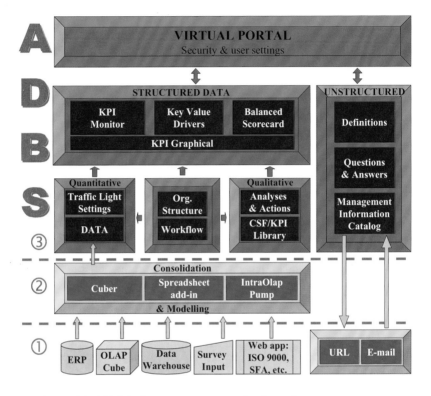

Figure 9.1: ADBS Architecture as an example of a performance management portal

Information transparency can be created throughout the organization by using a groupware-based intranet portal approach in the following way:

- Use the same look and feel of portal across divisions and business units to allow easy sharing of knowledge.

- Control access by effective security, within a common intranet, rather than by physically separating systems and intranets.

- Use the portal to provide business unit performance management home pages containing periodic management information such as Balanced Scorecards, financial (traffic light) reporting, forecasts, analysis, action reporting and strategic plans.

- Standardize these homepages across the organization to create a common, consistent and thereby user-friendly view of periodic management information.

- Provide drill-through to data warehouses and other management information systems across the organization from the portal to enable additional analysis and access to more detailed information.

- Use 'hyperlinks' to connect information in the portal to other web pages on the intranet and Internet, thereby connecting related information and enhancing the overall value of the information.

The benefits of a consistent portal approach are clear. Reports no longer have to be physically distributed. Users themselves access reports whenever they need them. Because a single user interface is used throughout the organization, no more time has to be put into translating data, and learning new tools. Subject to security, everybody has direct access to the (reporting) data of all organizational divisions, no matter where they are.

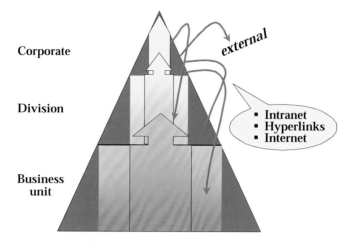

Figure 9.2: Management by surfing around

A portal facilitates 'management by surfing around' with a shift from copying databases towards staging results and providing 'linkages'. Instead of building a hierarchy of data warehouses, the portal brings together information and reports from many 'stand-alone' information systems and can provide links into the systems themselves. Linkages are internal as well as to external stakeholders' systems, for example, including customers and suppliers. The same implementation effort is re-used to deliver the same information to different communities of different users, each with its own security privileges. Given the right security privileges, management is free to access this information via the intranet and 'surf around'.

In Appendix D a checklist is given for the intranet delivery of management information and the Balanced Scorecard.

Case Study: Using technology at UltraViolet Design

One of Pete's favorite topics was reducing the cycle time from identifying a problem to resolving it. "Many business issues turn out to be about communication." is one of his favorite expressions.

*Another is, "If you **can** resolve it in real time, do resolve it in real time."*

Gary Williams was going through his management reports in ADBS. A small pop-up box in the bottom-right corner of his screen indicated that Sanch Panchis was trying to 'SameTime' conference with him.

The message said, "Gary, do you have a moment."

"Yes, reviewing reports but have time for you." responded Gary.

"I saw the new report for last month and saw that our margins were in the red zone in the traffic-light report. However, we were right on target last month according to our own accounting systems."

"So how are things going in Spain?" Gary typed.

"Are you on your normal number?" responded Sancho.

"No, in the UK office." replied Gary. A few moments later the phone rang and he picked up.

"Hi Gary, everything is muy bien in Spain," introduced Sancho, "but, as you've seen in my memo, the sales margin actuals from last month that we have differ from those in the UVD Balanced Scorecard."

"Let's see, I will bring up the screen now", Gary said as he opened the traffic light report. He looked under profitability and saw the Spanish figure.

"I presume that is also the reason that you didn't include an Action report yet?" Gary asked.

"That's right", Sancho said, "if you look at the figure in the traffic-light report, you see that it is straight on target. However, it is coded red, which would indicate that our margins are below target. Probably the target is set too high in the ADBS."

"You are right", replied Gary. "It's a numeric target rather than based on the budget we agreed. Sorry about that Sancho, I haven't updated it since our last meeting. I was pretty surprised

considering that you're the one who's normally on track. I'll make the necessary the change in the ADBS and you'll see that you have a green light. Take care, Sancho."

"Bye, Gary." Sancho said, much relieved.

Case Study: The new UltraViolet Design

Pete Fields drew up into the Visitor's parking space outside the UVD building before his summing-up meeting with John and Martin. As he pushed open the glass entrance door he was surprised to see the company vision statement etched over murals of parkland, rainforests and a subtle image of the world. Rosanna greeted Pete warmly and showed him how to sign in on the computerized visitor's register. He noticed she was looking at spreadsheets! Pete's nametag dropped from the printer and Rosanna show him to a seat.

"There is coffee in the machine, please help yourself," said Rosanna with a warm smile. "I'll just let John and Martin know you're here."

Pete smiled as Rosanna returned to her desk. He couldn't help noticing her welcome for everyone who came through the door. "What a change," he thought to himself.

John and Martin appeared a few minutes later and guided Pete to the conference room.

The brothers showed Pete the ADBS. Pete was pleased to see the screen was populated with Analysis and Actions. It was obviously being well used. Pete knew how important it was for John to see the Actions there – he had successfully created the transparency he was looking for.

"A lot of the numbers in the system are now fed directly from our ERP system and other systems. At first, we had to fill in a spreadsheet but that is almost all automated now," said John.

"That's great," replied Pete. "It's wonderful to see all the Objectives, Critical Success Factors and Key Performance Indicators in the system, too."

"What I like most," said John, "are the Actions! I can see at a glance everything that is being done to rectify problems. This

whole process has been amazing and the system is so flexible that adapting it to our changes is really easy."

"We wanted to meet you to show you our results and thank you for helping us to create our vision and plan during the past couple of months. Without your coaching a lot of what you see at UVD now would not have been possible."

"We know that we had a lot to do with what has happened but without you it just wouldn't have turned out this way. And we know that there is still a lot of work to do," continued Martin. "But we now have a clear direction and a path to follow. You made a big difference here."

"I'm excited by the results we have achieved so far. We are solving problems and creating new opportunities faster and with an ease we've never experienced before. It is very energizing."

"Wow," said Pete. "I didn't expect this today. Let me just say that it is wonderful to be a part of a company that is so clearly doing a good job for its customers, its employees and the planet. Well done."

Section 3: Applying the ideas in this book

10. IMPLEMENTING THE PERFORMANCE MANAGEMENT HABITS

KEY POINTS

☑ The Performance Management Process is largely the same across organizations.

☑ Configure don't customize to deliver in weeks not months.

☑ The Action Driven Balanced Scorecard shows how the Habits can be supported

☑ Start simple to get immediate management benefits.

☑ Don't try to figure it all out in advance – get started and let the system learn.

☑ Integration comes after configuring and making the system work, not before.

☑ Don't forget to manage buy-in.

Configure, don't customize

With the relentless speed of the New Economy, organizations can no longer afford long, risky, expensive, custom development projects or restrictive proprietary solutions. Why should every organization have to re-invent the wheel, when the basic performance management process is the same across organizations and particularly within industry sectors?

The Action Driven Balanced Scorecard (ADBS) is an example of a Performance Management Portal, jointly developed by Lotus/Show Business and Arthur Andersen Business Consulting, to be configured quickly and at low cost. ADBS has two major components: the Balanced Scorecard with corrective actions and the MI Catalog, a report and knowledge catalog, with workflow to help administrators to continually improve the information available by responding to requests. ADBS has the Habits built-in. ADBS also includes Frequently Asked Questions and Definitions of Terms that can be replaced or added to by users and Administrators as ADBS is used.

The MI Catalog can be configured with categorizations for information in the Catalog to define departmental structures, user groups, etc within a particular organization. At a deeper level, the workflow that turns requests from users into new MI Catalog entries can also be configured.

Immediately after it is configured, ADBS can be used. Initially, entries in the MI Catalog can be made manually. User requests automatically point to the most important gaps. The Balanced Scorecard within ADBS can be updated manually in the first instance and populated automatically from business systems over time. An initial Balanced Scorecard design can be changed and evolved in response to user feedback.

Implementing the Habits

In this section we briefly describe how each Habit is supported by the ADBS system.

Habit 1: Deliver on the strategy and goals

The vision and theory of performance management is easier to describe than it is to implement. In a large organization there are typically many performance management needs.

ADBS provides a framework for relating strategy to CSFs to KPIs and presenting the results as a Balanced Scorecard that shows each person the KPIs and corrective actions that they are entitled to see.

In any Balanced Scorecard project, one problem is that often, non-financial key performance cannot be calculated from the ERP system or the Data Warehouse. The data may be in many different systems, for example a competency profiling system, an ISO 9000 system, a web survey or a Lotus Notes workflow. All of these different sources of data may be running on different networks at different locations. Bringing all of the information together can be a significant challenge – both in terms of collecting data and turning data into the KPIs which are needed to monitor progress.

Because ADBS uses Lotus Notes and Domino, the interfacing challenges are significantly reduced. Summary data from any of these sources can be automatically and dependably delivered into a Lotus Notes or Domino database which means that, without replacing all its existing systems, an organization can bring together the data needed to calculate its KPIs and hence evaluate performance against strategy. Lotus Notes and Domino are used to securely capture data for ADBS. Creating KPIs from any of these data sources requires consolidation (to aggregate results to a meaningful level) and modelling (to create ratios and metrics rather than just sums). Cuber is the consolidation and modelling engine that creates KPIs for use in ADBS.

Anyone in an organization who can access Lotus Notes, the intranet or Internet can see and use the performance management information which they need to do their job. ADBS documents and presents the relationships between strategic aims, critical success factors and key performance indicators, for example in the KPI Monitor screen (see Figure 10.1).

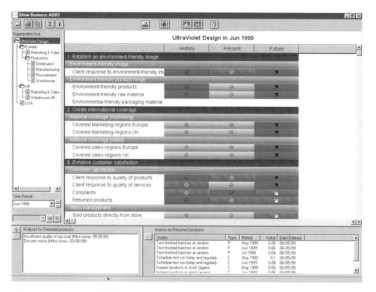

Figure 10.1: The KPI Monitor shows relation between Mission, Objectives, CSFs and KPIs.

Habit 2: Create and manage internal partnership

ADBS manages the security and access rules to show people only the scorecards and KPIs within scorecards which they are entitled to see. The result is that people can look at the same strategies, the same KPIs and the same definitions, wherever they are. This means that the WHY, WHAT, HOW from the organization's perspective is clear.

A Performance Management Portal in itself cannot design a purpose or vision for an organization. What it can do is to provide a framework inside which each person has *a line of sight* to see how their own objectives and measures relate to the objectives and measures of the organization. This line or sight means that anyone can see what they are contributing to the overall result at any time. To empower individuals and give thrust to the organization, the purpose, vision, plan and action must be kept alive. From a business perspective everyone must be able to see the performance management information which they need to play their role. Meetings, conference calls and conversations are centred around ADBS, using the WHY and WHAT, in order to determine the HOW. The groupware/intranet technology on which ADBS is based means that it can support the whole team, whether the team size is 20 or 20,000 people. ADBS is a shared knowledge base, to which everyone can contribute and from which everyone can learn – a virtual meeting place.

The ADBS system captures the WHY, WHAT, HOW context on which internal partnership is built and maintained.

People can work together, supported with the same information and context from different physical locations and time zones. By removing barriers of scale, time and place, a Performance Management Portal removes practical barriers to creating and managing internal partnership. Yes, it can be deployed across a small department or a large distributed enterprise, but the best performance management system, the best technology, the best strategy, will not be successful without a Paradigm of partnership.

Habit 3: Keep it simple

The ADBS system makes it simple to report on Key Value Drivers (KVDs) in budgeting, reporting and forecasting, via Lotus Notes or intranet. The ADBS provides a seamless view into all of the parts of the performance management process:

- *Strategy* is represented as the hierarchy of strategic objectives and KVDs. Also, strategic action plans are collected and made available to the organization in the MI Catalog section of the ADBS.

- *Budgeting* results provide the targets that are used to compare with actuals and forecasts for exception reporting in the Balanced Scorecards.

- *Reporting* on performance is delivered in the Balanced Scorecards and Action Reports.

- *Forecasting* also feeds Balanced Scorecards and Action Reports.
- *Incentive Compensation* is made effective by using the ADBS to show people what is important and how they are performing against targets.

Habit 4: Manage by exception

In ADBS, exception conditions can be defined and maintained using simple rules relating actual performance to, for example, last month, last year, or a target value. These rules can be applied across an enterprise, for example to monitor a certain level of Return On Capital Employed, or overridden by an individual organization unit to take into account the particular sector or market in which that business unit works. This means that the manager can measure him/herself based on more demanding exception conditions, so that s/he can see and correct problems before they become exceptions for higher levels of management. ADBS automatically calculates KPI values from ERP systems' or operational data, and from information gathered from around the enterprise. Then, exceptions are highlighted automatically in the Balanced Scorecard and traffic light screens. Exceptions are identified by color and symbol in a table of results, which can be related to contingencies in the ADBS. Face to face and teleconference meetings can review these exception reports to analyse issues and decide on corrective actions. The exception screen, which the ADBS displays to a particular team, is dependent on their role and position in the organization. The ADBS automatically shows individuals the exception report that is important to them and gives them access to other exception reports to which they have security access. The ADBS helps people throughout the organization to manage by exception.

Habit 5: Manage by action

While organizations register data from every purchase and every transaction, actions that are critical to survival and fulfillment of strategy are often relegated to meeting minutes, private workbooks, to-do lists and Post-it™ Notes. ADBS captures corrective actions, preventative actions and breakthrough actions, providing a secure management resource for reviewing who is doing what, why they are doing it and how much of the goal has been achieved. The ADBS system tracks actions from an initial request, through acceptance, planning, implementation and completion. The actions that each person sees depends on their security rights and privileges. ADBS is more than a shared to-do list, because each action is stored against the strategy, CSFs and KPIs to which it relates. The creator of the action has to think about WHY before they define WHAT and HOW. Once the action is created, its strategic significance is continually reinforced by the strategy, the CSFs and the KPIs that are a part of its definition.

Habit 6: Create information transparency

ADBS is a Performance Management Portal that has been developed to provide best practice based on all of the requirements described above, including combining information from many different sources.

Just as there can be one centralized data warehouse for storing data and many smaller local data-marts in different organizations, ADBS can be used in a centralized or distributed way. There might be one ADBS for each separate organization unit, which is used to provide Balanced Scorecards for all of the businesses within that organization unit with secure, but transparent access for everyone within the organization. The headquarters might have its own ADBS with only the top level scorecards for divisions, but have the ability to access some or all of the performance management information for lower levels in the organization. Alternatively, there might be a single ADBS for the entire organization with security settings to determine which information can be seen by different people in different business units.

ADBS provides a portal for critical success factors, key performance indicators, Balanced Scorecards, actions, reports from business intelligence systems and other knowledge relating to performance management. As a Domino application, ADBS can also be replicated, which means that a copy of ADBS and the information that it contains can be transferred onto a remote laptop computer and updated when email is updated (by replication). Replication also means that a copy of the headquarters ADBS can be replicated to a local intranet for one of the divisions, to allow instant access to up-to-date information, even when there is no fast intranet or network link between the division and headquarters.

ADBS provides a mechanism whereby a user who cannot find the information they require can request it from an Administrator. This request is then routed through a workflow process to Administrators. Administrators can see all requests pending and so manage them effectively. Users can track the status of their own requests. To respond to a request, an Administrator can add a report to the MI Catalog, or arrange for an external reporting tool to regularly update the report in the Catalog. Each Report has a 'sell-by-date'. Normally it will be updated automatically. If it is not, then the Administrators will be informed when it is about to pass its sell-by-date, then it will be removed from the Catalog. As requests are met and new entries are added to the Catalog, users can help themselves to what they need, so Administrators have the time to improve the system and the organization learns.

ADBS consists of Lotus Notes databases that can be used by any Lotus Notes user, whether they are working on an aeroplane, or connected to the organization's intranet. ADBS can be used to deliver performance management information from any system or project to users anywhere.

Habit 7: Leverage technology

Every organization has a rich array of technology components that are the result of significant investment in time and money. In most cases, they do a good job. The performance management system should add value to these, rather than needing to replace them. All of the enterprise integration tools for Lotus Notes and Domino mean that ADBS can use data for Balanced Scorecard KPIs from virtually any source. In addition to the structured KPI data supplied by these sources, ADBS also stages reports and documents from other systems and reporting tools in the MI Catalog. One of the most popular standards for report delivery from reporting tools is email. Any reporting tool that can send an email can add a report to the MI Catalog in ADBS. In addition IBM's MQ Series can deliver data from virtually any source, including legacy systems.

Calculating KPI values for ADBS

There are a number of approaches by which KPI values can be calculated for ADBS from source data:

- One approach is to bring all of the source data together in a performance management relational data-mart or data warehouse and then to calculate the KPIs from the combined table of data. This calculation can be performed by an OLAP database or the Cuber product, which is a consolidation engine which can work within a Lotus Domino server.

- A second approach is to combine the different sources of data in an OLAP database, which can then perform sophisticated calculations to produce KPI values.

- Alternately, source data can be gathered from remote sources and systems into Notes/Domino databases and replicated to a central location, where KPIs can be calculated from the Notes data by Cuber.

- The simplest approach is to structure the KPI values in a spreadsheet and use the spreadsheet add-in, which works with ADBS, to push the data into ADBS.

Because the Notes/Domino infrastructure solves so many of the traditional issues of enterprise performance management, we recommend that organizations consider the collaboration and co-ordination capabilities of Lotus Notes/Domino for their performance management portal, even if they do not use it for email. Given this foundation, we can now consider how to leverage other technology in combination with Notes/Domino to deliver a performance management portal.

Lotus Notes and Domino do not natively provide for the specific best practice requirements of presenting a Balanced Scorecard, charting and tabulating data and traffic lighting exceptions.

The 'Show Business' toolset is an extension of Lotus Notes and Domino on which ADBS is based. It has been developed over several years alongside the Notes/Domino products to allow Notes/Domino to work elegantly with quantitative data like that found in a Balanced Scorecard. Without it, ADBS, or any other portal based on Notes and Domino, could not manage the quantitative data and presentation requirements of a Balanced Scorecard.

The combination of Notes/Domino and the Show Business toolset provides the building blocks of the ADBS server and user interface.

Integration through standard interfaces

Standard interfaces mean that the ADBS system can use data from virtually any data source including:

- ERP systems from suppliers like SAP, JD Edwards, SSA, Lawson, etc .

- OLAP and consolidation systems like Hyperion Enterprise, Essbase, ShowCase, Oracle Express, Cognos PowerCube and TM1.

- relational databases like UDB, DB2 and Oracle.

- spreadsheets - if an organization already has a Balanced Scorecard design, then a 'quick win' can be achieved by entering the scorecard data into a spreadsheet and transferring it directly into ADBS.

- and Lotus Domino applications including surveys, ISO 9000 and Sales Force Automation systems. Reports for the MI Catalog can be received from virtually any reporting tool via email. Further details of interfaces and a sample spreadsheet

template for populating ADBS is available on
www.showbusiness.com. (Appendix E includes an
architecture diagram for ADBS.)

Implementation steps

Successful implementation of any performance management system requires building of commitment – creating buy-in.

Even if there is commitment to the concept of enterprise performance management, different people have different ideas about how to make it happen.

Broadly, there are three phases to delivering a successful solution:

- **Preparation** – understanding the strategy to be supported, the interest groups, the information sources and creating a plan from start to finish.

- **Pilot** – delivering a solution to a chosen sub-set of potential users and creating business value for that target group.

- **Rollout** – extending the results of a successful pilot across multiple departments, organization units or networked organizations.

As each of these phases is implemented a wider community of people needs to buy-in and provide support.

Other considerations

The Habits and practices described in this book suggest useful principles, but clearly they are not recipes for success. The ADBS provides a useful framework, but implementing it does not guarantee best practice performance management. The right process requires leadership to make it work and technology to support it.

To implement a standard performance management process across a large organization, it is useful to ask the following questions:

- Is it possible to create a meaningful set of standard indicators for the entire organization, given the level of diversity and complexity of the organizational units involved?

- Can these indicators be consolidated in a meaningful way? Do they have to be consolidated?

- Does corporate and divisional management need non-financial indicators to manage the business, considering their current management control style? Should the financial only management style be reviewed?

- Can the strategic, financial and operational measures be related to one another without creating complexity rather than clarity?

By including non-financial information in the performance management process, managers can get a fuller picture of the performance of the organization. They can identify and deal with issues before they become problems, making it possible to respond more quickly to changing circumstances. However, it is important to find the right balance between non-financial and financial information. When an organization's main focus is on non-financial information, there is the risk of managers losing track of the financial bottom line.

Full circle: from technical implementation and back to buy-in

Improving performance management requires a self-improvement culture, yet to support improvement of culture, we need good performance management. This is a chicken-and-egg situation. Where do we start? Introducing action-oriented reporting (with review meetings and accountabilities) will start to change culture. However, to introduce it in the first place will require buy-in from the people who need to make it work. This brings us back to where we started: to implement best practice performance management, we need to take into account process, technology and people issues.

Change requires buy-in. From beginning to end we must create and manage internal partnership in order to deliver effective change.

11. PROFESSIONAL SUPPORT

The companies and authors who are responsible for this book and the ADBS system are described in this chapter. You will find a directory of world-wide contacts for the ADBS solution and related business and technical integration services at www.showbusiness.com.

Arthur Andersen Business Consulting

Arthur Andersen Business Consulting is part of Arthur Andersen, one of world's largest multi-disciplinary professional services firms. Arthur Andersen provides client service through assurance, business consulting, economic & financial consulting and tax, legal & business advisory services. More than 60,000 employees are working in 382 offices in 81 countries. Arthur Andersen is based on the 'one-firm' concept: the organization acts as a single firm on areas of quality assurance, research and development, exchange of know-how and training of partners and employees.

A modern organization continuously anticipates changing requirements and circumstances. Arthur Andersen Business Consulting assists leading organizations to improve their decision making, business operations and organizational capability through a broad range of process improvement, performance enhancement and technology implementation services. Using proprietary tools such as the Arthur Andersen Knowledge Space[SM] and the Global Best Practices[SM] knowledge base, Arthur Andersen Business Consulting provides creative insights and implements practical business solutions to help clients world-wide achieve measurable performance improvement and lasting change.

The consultants of Arthur Andersen Business Consulting work towards providing integral solutions, integrating their experience with process restructuring, analysis and redesign of organizations, improvement of management reporting and information processes, implementation of reporting information systems, project management and change enablement. In close co-operation with the client, expectations are exceeded and deadlines are met in such a way that results are measurable and lasting.

Show Business

Show Business' products combine best practice management models, cultural change and e-business technologies to enable high performance organizations. Show Business develops configurable intranet and groupware performance management tools and Balanced Scorecard solutions. The company provides these performance monitoring and measurement tools to corporations world-wide through business consultancy partnerships, IBM, Lotus and business partners as well as through independent software vendors. Through its partnerships, Show Business supports organizational leaders and change agents in implementing organizations which deliver measurable, positive outcomes for them and their stakeholders (including shareholders, employees, customers and the community). For information on relationships with ERP vendors, other independent software vendors and implementation partners, visit www.showbusiness.com which provides a secure forum for sharing best-practice, benchmarking and networking. Contact:

Show Business
137 Euston Road
London NW1 2AA
England

Phone: +44-(0)20 -7387-3888
Fax: +44-(0)20 -7387-3883
email: BSC@Showbusiness.com

Lotus Development Corporation

Lotus Development Corp. is the undisputed global leader in messaging, collaboration and Knowledge Management solutions that enable corporations of all sizes to communicate, collaborate, share knowledge and conduct business via the Internet. In 1989, Lotus revolutionized the way networked knowledge workers collaborate when it introduced the concept of groupware with the launch of Lotus Notes.

Over the past few years, the market for collaboration has exploded, quadrupling since 1995. A prime catalyst behind this growth has been the phenomenal growth of the Internet and the World Wide Web. Lotus launched the Domino server in June 1996, bringing complete Internet standardization to Lotus Notes at the server level.

Today, Lotus is leveraging its rapidly broadening margin of leadership in collaboration by standardizing its entire product set - from Notes and Domino to LearningSpace and SmartSuite - on open Internet protocols to allow businesses world-wide to profitably work the Web with "Super Human" precision and speed.

With the latest release of Lotus Domino Release 5 (R5), Lotus once again leads the industry in dramatically shifting the dynamics of how business is conducted on a global basis. With all of its products and services, Lotus is driving development of solutions that are harnessing the power of the Internet to provide customers' enterprise-wide Knowledge Management to achieve real-world corporate and organizational objectives.

Visit www.lotus.com or contact Coen_Baarslag@lotus.com.

The authors

André de Waal

André de Waal is Partner of Arthur Andersen Business Consulting. He graduated in chemistry (Leiden, 1983), in Business Administration (Northeastern University, Boston, 1985) and is certified in Production and Inventory Management (American Production and Inventory Control Society, 1993). Since he started his career with Arthur Andersen in 1986, André has gained a lot of experience: with the selection and implementation of production, logistic and financial software packages; with re-engineering and streamlining business processes; with cost analyses; with designing logistic concepts and information technology infrastructures; and with the implementation of critical success factors and key performance indicators. In several of these projects, he worked on international assignments, most recently on a benchmark study for a Dutch multinational performed in Japan, Germany and the USA. He is the co-author of numerous articles and of four books on the topic of performance management. André can be contacted at:

P.O. Box 21937   Phone: +31-10-880-1400
3001 AX Rotterdam   Fax: +31-10-880-1616
The Netherlands   email: andre.de.waal@
                                  nl.arthur andersen.com

Morel Fourman

Morel Fourman is one of the founders and the CEO of Show Business. He is passionate about the importance of performance management in creating organizations which harness the purpose, potential and commitment of people. Morel works with senior executives, coaches project champions and leads workshops on breaking through the business, cultural and technology challenges of high performance. Morel has 14 years experience in designing performance management solutions and has been responsible for client solutions in the UK, Europe and USA. Morel graduated from Balliol College Oxford in 1982 and took a Masters degree specializing in computer-aided design and artificial intelligence. For questions relating to this book, Morel can be contacted through Show Business via the email address NewEconomy@showbusiness.com

Appendices

Appendix A. Literature

Arthur Andersen Business Consulting, World Class Performance
Management, results of international benchmark study, Arthur
Andersen The Netherlands, 1999

Bambauer, E.E. , Scorecarding Your Future: eMeasures, Basis Point
Newsletter for the asset management industry, Spring 1999

Brancato, C.K., New corporate performance measures, The
Conference Board, Report 1118-95-RR, 1995

Business Intelligence Research, Performance measures, the new
agenda, 1993

Campbell, D., If you don't know where you're going, you'll probably
end up somewhere else, Tabor Publishing, 1974

Case, John, Open-Book Management, Harper Business, 1995

Case, John, The Open-Book Management Experience, Addison-
Wesley, 1998

Charan, R., G. Colvin, Why CEOs fail, Fortune, June 21, 1999

Christopher, W.F. (ed.), New management accounting, Crisp
Management Library, 1998

Collins, J.C., Parras, J.I., Built to Last, Harper Collins,1994

Connelly, R., R. McNeill, R. Mosimann, The multidimensional
manager, 24 ways to impact your bottom line in 90 days, Cognos
Incorporated, 1997

Connors, R., T. Smith, Journey to the emerald city, Prentice Hall
Press, 1999

Currie, W.L., B. Galliers (ed.), Rethinking management information
systems, Oxford University Press, 1999

Donovan, J., R. Tully, B. Wortman, The value enterprise, McGraw-
Hill, 1997

His Holiness the Dalai Lama, Ancient Wisdom Modern World, Little
Brown Book Company, London, 1999

Drucker, P.F., What information do executives need?, Financial
Times, April 19th, 1999

Drucker, P.F., Management challenges for the 21st century, Harper Business, 1999

Fisher, Ury, Patten, Getting to Yes, Penguin

Frankl, V.E., Man's Search for Meaning, Simon & Schuster, 1984

Gates, B., Business @ the speed of thought, using a digital nervous system, Penguin Books, 1999

Gooderham, G., B.H. Maskell, Information systems that support performance management, Journal of Strategic Performance Measurement, February/March 1998

Goold, M., A. Campbell, M. Alexander, Corporate level strategy, creating value in the multibusiness company, John Wiley & Sons, 1994

Goss, T., The Last Word on Power, Doubleday, 1996

Hartman, Amir and Sifonis, John, Net Ready, strategies for success in the e-conomy, McGraw Hill, 1999

Haskins, M.E., B.R. Makela (ed.), The CFO handbook, Irwin, 1997

Holtham, C., Integrating technologies to support action, City University Business School, London, 1994

Hope, J., R. Fraser, Beyond budgeting …, building a new managerial model for the information age, CAM-I, 1998

Hope, J., R. Fraser, Budgets: the hidden barriers to success in the information age, Accounting & Business, March 24, 1999

Hope, J., R. Fraser, Budgets: how to manage without them, Accounting & Business, April 30, 1999

Inmon, W.H., C. Imhoff, R. Sousa, Corporate Information Factory, Wiley Computer Publishing, 1998

Johnson, H.T., R.S. Kaplan, Relevance lost, Harvard Business School Press, 1987/92

Johnson, H.T., Relevance regained, Free Press, 1992

Kaplan, R.S., D.P. Norton, The Balanced Scorecard, Harvard Business School Press, 1996

Kelly, K., Out of Control, Addison Wesley, 1994

Knight, J.A., Value based management, developing a systematic approach to creating shareholder value, McGraw-Hill, 1998

Koln, A., Punished by Rewards, Houghton Mifflin, 1993

Kröger, F., M. Träm, M. Vandenbosch, Spearheading growth, how Europe's top companies are restructuring to win, Pitman Publishing, 1998

Lazere, C., All together now, why you must link budgeting and forecasting to planning and performance, CFO Magazine, February 1998

McAuliffe, T.P., C.S. Shamlin, Critical Information Network, 1992

McKinnon, S.M., W.J. Bruns Jr., The Information Mosaic, 1992

Merchant, K.A., Modern management systems, Prentice Hall, 1998

Olve, N.G., J. Roy, M. Wetter, Performance drivers, a practical guide to using the Balanced Scorecard, John Wiley & Sons, 1999

Papows, J., Enterprise.com, market leadership in the information ages, Nicholas Brealey Publishing, 1999

Redwood, S., C. Goldwasser, S. Street, Action management, practical strategies for making your corporate transformation a success, John Wiley & Sons, 1999

Renaissance Solution Limited, Translating strategy into action, research rapport, 1996

Roddick, A., Body and Soul, Ebury Press, 1991

Schiemann, W. and Associates, Executive measurement management survey, American Management Association, 1996

Serven, L.B.M., Value planning, the new approach to building value every day, John Wiley & Sons, 1998

Simon, W.L., Beyond the numbers, how leading companies measure and drive success, VNR, 1997

Waal, A.A. de, H. Bulthuis, Managementrapportage is kunst! (*'Management Reporting is an Art'*), Tijdschrift Financieel Management, 1997/5

Waal, A.A. de, J.H.J.M. Mijland-Bessems, H. Bulthuis, Meten Moet! (*'Measurement is a Must'*), Kluwer BedrijfsInformatie, 1998

Waal, A.A. de, H. Bulthuis, Actie is alles (*'Action is Everything'*), Kluwer BedrijfsInformatie, 1999

Walther, T., H. Johansson, J. Dunleavy, E. Hjelm, Reinventing the CFO, McGraw-Hill, 1997

Wheatley, Margaret J., Leadership and the New Science, Berrett-Koehler Publishers, Inc., 1994

Appendix B. Management Information and Reporting Analysis self-assessment

Description of the MIRA

High-quality management information and reporting is a very important part of the performance management process. In order to assess the quality and the use of the management information and reporting function in an organization, we developed the Management Information and Reporting Analysis (MIRA) which consists of the following elements:

- assessment of an organization's internal reporting (for use of managers), external reporting (for use of shareholders, banks, etc.) is not considered;

- examination of the reporting and communication tools that are used;

- examination of the availability of information (financial and non-financial data relating to mission statement, strategy and critical business functions;

- assessment of the reliability, timeliness and layout of information in management reports;

- review of the use of management information in the performance management process.

In the MIRA, the eight aspects are rated on a scale ranging from A to E. For each aspect, the organization's performance is compared to the performance of best practice companies throughout the world. If the examined organization meets most of the criteria, the score on this aspect is rated an A. The less 'best practice' criteria are met, the lower the score is. Score E means that the organization's reporting really needs improvement on the aspect in question. Score C means that the performance regarding this meets 40 to 60 percent of the criteria for a best practice organisation in that aspect.

The MIRA has been performed at fifty organizations worldwide. These organizations varied in size (small and big), organizational structure (holdings and independent companies) and industry (profit and not-for-profit organizations). The following radar diagram presents the average score of the fifty organizations graphically. For clarity, note that an organization with best practice performance management in all respects would score A for all aspects. The average organization scores only D or E for 'Non Financials', because, for that aspect, most companies are much worse than best practice.

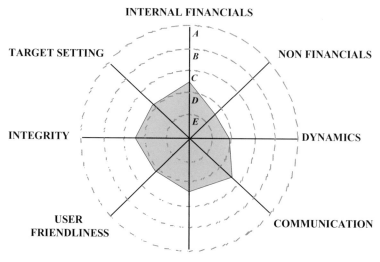

Figure B.1: MIRA Radar Diagram, average result

Most organizations are weak on Non-Financials and Dynamics.

Few organizations score better than C on more than 2 aspects. Main positive points are found in MIRAs for fifty organizations:

- Use of financial budgets, which are specific to departments and products.
- Reports used for making decisions and defining actions to improve future results.
- Managers are well informed about the organization's mission and strategy.
- Many have improvement plans for the management reporting function.
- Increased attention is being paid to optimizing the use of information technology.
- Reported figures are highly reliable.
- Managers accepting targets and using them for evaluating results.

Common opportunities for improvement are:

- Include more financial ratios.
- Include non-financial critical success factors and key performance indicators, to monitor the degree to which strategic objectives are being attained.
- Define clearer accountability for the results of key performance indicators.
- Focus attention on analysis of results.
- Make reports more action and future oriented.
- Link the reporting system directly to the operational systems that generate the data, thereby decreasing the need for manual intervention.
- Increase the user-friendliness of management reports, for example by decreasing the volume.

- Use more formal approaches to setting targets (for example, based on benchmark figures of other organizations).

MIRA recommendations

On the basis of the MIRAs a number of recommendations can be made, of which the main ones are listed below. It is not a complete list, and other recommendations can be made as well.

Recommendation:
Improve formal steering and control tools

Many organizations do not have the management information to rigorously manage based on quantitative measures of performance. If there is relevant quantitative information, not everyone who needs it gets it. There are not standard reporting layouts for reports or scheduled meetings to review them. As a consequence, managers may make decisions without consideration and rigor. Quantitative information is used for accountability (looking back at what happened), but not for steering – to effect what will happen. In the absence of formal performance management information and process, informal and qualitative information is the only fall back.

Best practice organizations use a combination of formal and informal steering and control tools, with strong emphasis on the formal measures and disciplines. In these organizations, formal information is always supplemented by qualitative information, often from informal sources. This is because information like, for example, newswire reports, opinions and economic trends are not delivered as numbers. Formal steering and control can be improved significantly by implementing a performance management process based on the Habits described in this book. Key requirements are a standardized reporting set, planned reporting meetings, and use of flexible IT support.

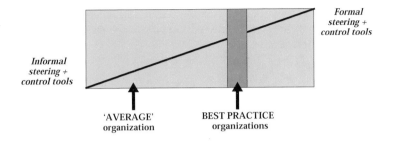

Formal
steering +
control tools

Informal
steering +
control tools

'AVERAGE'
organization

BEST PRACTICE
organizations

Figure B.2: The balance between formal and informal control tools

Recommendation:
Include non-financial information in reports

Strategy can be forgotten because there is no explicit relationship between the strategy of the organization and the reports being provided. Many management reports focus predominantly on financial data. One of the disadvantages of this financial focus is that figures are merely a reflection of past results ('lagging information'). 'Leading indicators' like measures of customer satisfaction, capacity to innovate and organizational flexibility are often missing entirely.

By including non-financial information, managers get a better insight into what is going on in the organization and what outcomes will be produced in the future. They can anticipate problems and act more quickly than they could with only past-based financial measures. It is important to find the right balance between non-financial and financial information.

Recommendation:
Formulate the role of management in steering on results.

Often management information does not relate to the real business needs of managers, for example because those managers were not involved in defining it.

The management team needs a clear understanding of its role in implementing strategy and a definition of its in controlling and steering based on management reports. Management reporting must align with and reinforce strategy and provide organization-wide (not merely departmental) information.

Recommendation:
Implement performance action management.
To measure performance just for the sake of measurement is not very useful. Managers need to turn their insights into action to effect events and create value. In many organizations, there was no formal process for turning measures issues and problems into actions. This process is described **as** performance **action management**. Most reports are designed to report results, not to monitor actions. Ideally reports should include forecasts. **Performance action management** requires a culture of openness and self-improvement – correction not blame. This culture is supported and reinforced by management information that incorporate future-oriented information and can measure and monitor actions.

Recommendation:
Align and integrate the performance management process.
A general improvement opportunity from the MIRAs is the need for *integration* of the steps in the performance management process. Alignment of the information used and created by each step in the performance management process can increases transparency, reduce costs and increase effectiveness.

Perform your own MIRA
The MIRA asks questions which focus attention on important management reporting issues. To perform your own MIRA, visit www.showbusiness.com.

Appendix C. Checklist for performance management portal

A management information catalog provides a one-stop-shop for information from multiple sources. Here is a quick checklist of requirements. How well does the package provide each of the following?

- Delivery of reports from all existing systems.
- Cataloging reports and information in relation to strategy.
- Process support for continual improvement of reports vs. simple report publishing.
- Business intelligence roles for different parts of reporting process.
- Request/workflow support for reporting (co-ordination).
- Security (data driven).
- Adequate scalability with manageability.
- Off-line working and replication to different intranets.
- Acceptable cost of ownership - more documents, more users.
- Integration with existing reporting tools.
- Support for manual entries.

A Balanced Scorecard has different meanings in different organizations but, essentially, it provides an overview summary of measures from different perspectives of the organization. Here is a quick checklist of requirements. How well does the package provide each of the following?

- Management of strategy and organization structure.
- Personalized Balanced Scorecard depending on role, organizational position and security privileges.
- Action support, tracking and workflow.

- Easy to understand exception boundaries – for defining of traffic light exceptions.
- Capture qualitative or 'soft' information and knowledge.
- Security (data driven).
- Adequate scalability with manageability.
- Off-line working and replication to different intranets.
- Link to ERP, operational systems, data warehouses and OLAP databases.
- Links to quality, help-desk, sales force applications.
- Manual data entry, customer and employee surveys.

Appendix D. Criteria for package selection

When selecting an information system to support the performance management process in your organization in an efficient and effective way, the following criteria can be useful.

Performance Management Criteria

1. Strategy CSF/KPI Reporting:

- Balanced Scorecard – Can the package support the display formats you require?

- Document strategy – Does the package allow you to document your strategy?

- Document cross-organization KPIs – Does the package allow for sharing of KPI definitions across the organization and unique KPI definitions for individual organization units?

- Capture of soft metrics – Does the package allow for capture of metrics from survey tools, ISO 9000 systems, etc?

- Reports from other systems – Does the package allow publishing of reports from other systems that you need to report from (including desktop OLAP tools, ERP systems, data warehouse, operational systems, legacy systems, etc)?

2. Key Value Driver Reporting:

- Subset selection (Key Value Drivers) – Does the package allow you to focus on a subset of KPIs which drive value, without excluding other KPIs from the overall system which also need to be tracked?

- KPI calculation from source data – Does the package support calculation of KPIs (ratios, percentages, etc) from source data, either internally, or by using an external OLAP database?

- Organizational drill-down – Does the package allow drill-down the organization hierarchy?

3. Internal Partnership Support:

- Can everything be personalized: Scorecards, Key Value Drivers, presentation displays and actions?
- Can measures in the package be related to the strategy?
- Does the security of the package allow privacy as well as transparency?
- Does the package document WHY, WHAT and HOW?

4. Exception Reporting:

- Flexible exception settings – Does the package allow definition of rules for exception reporting of each KPI, both across the organization and specifically for a business unit?
- How easy can exception boundaries across organization units be specified?
- Does the package use traffic lighting based on exception boundaries?
- Can exception boundaries be different by organization unit and KPI?

5. Action Management:

- Action reports hyperlinked to Balanced Scorecard – Does the package allow drill-down from Balanced Scorecard to detailed information and activity for the KPI?
- Commentary, Analysis – Do these details include analysis, or commentary to allow collaboration and shared learning?
- Corrective Action and Preventative Action management (workflow) – Does the package support definition and tracking of corrective actions and can corrective action workflow

integrate with the messaging and groupware standards of the organization?

- Action Reports combine chart/data with KPI Header, Analysis and Actions – Does the Action Report provide all of the information required to know WHO, WHEN, WHY, WHAT and HOW for the KPI?

6. Information transparency:

- Ease of use for end users – Is the package easy to use for end users?

- Ease of deployment – locations, networks, users – How easy is it to deploy the package to networked, disconnected and mobile users?

- Scorecard functionality – Does the Scorecard document exception boundaries?

- Inclusion of report objects from any source – Does the package allow inclusion of reports from other systems? How is this automated?

- Manual report addition – Can reports be added manually?

- Web/intranet delivery – Can these reports be published by intranet?

- Data and role dependent security – Is data, role and organization unit based security supported?

- Workflow for user requests and additions – Does the package support workflow for requesting and improving the information content?

- Enterprise security model – Can the package use the existing security and sign-on?

- Easy maintenance/security – If a separate security system is required, is it easy to maintain and will it scale to every user in the organization? If not, how far will it scale and are you sure that that is enough?

- Organizational unit related rights – Does the package allow organizational units to 'own' their own implementation, but still provide secure access to people in other parts of the organization?

7. Leverage technology:

- Use of existing naming/security – See above.
- Use of existing hardware – Will the package require deployment of more hardware?
- Use of existing software – To what extent does the package use existing software: OLAP databases, data warehouse?
- Use of existing intranet/groupware – To what extent does the package use hardware, network bandwidth and server processing power, provided for intranet and groupware?
- ERP system data – Can the package use data from the ERP system(s) in use in the organization? What facility is provided for collecting data from remote and multiple ERP systems?
- Operational systems data – What links are available for operational systems data?
- Data warehouse data – What links are available for data warehouse data?
- OLAP data feeds – What links are available for OLAP database data?
- Web data capture (or groupware) – What facilities are provided for Web or groupware survey and data capture?
- KPI calculation – What facilities are provided for KPI calculation and can these be replaced by best of breed (OLAP and modelling) tools?
- Surf data – Can the user 'surf' across data from different KPIs and organization units, subject to security?
- Drill-down – Can the user drill-down to detail?

- Operating systems and platform support (client and server) – Are the preferred operating systems supported for client and server?

Implementation Criteria

1. Ease of getting started:

- How easy is the configuration (for instance, of the scorecard)?
- How easy is source data access?
- How easy is KPI calculation?
- How easy is integration (for instance, with reporting tools)?
- Suitable for tactical and strategic use – Can the package start small and scale to every user?

2. Flexibility to organization development and change:

- Can the package support the changing of the strategy/CSFs/KPIs easily?
- Can the package support the change in an individual's role easily?
- Can the package support the change in security classification of information easily?
- Can the package be implemented at multiple locations?
- Tactical implementation possible – Can the package be implemented as a quick win within one division, without limiting future scope for wider use?

3. Financial Considerations:

- What are the costs in the first year?
- What is the total cost of ownership of the package, (including software, hardware, configuration, installation, training, additional maintenance and additional support)?

Appendix E. Technical architecture of the ADBS system

The ADBS system is a virtual portal for best practice performance management. It is a portal because it lets any user participate in the performance management process by providing a one-stop-shop for information from many different systems, presenting Balanced Scorecards and staging reports, knowledge, performance management information and action workflow in Lotus Notes or a Domino server. It is virtual, because it supports users in distributed teams, including mobile workers even when there is no permanent physical connection between groups of users and between users and information sources. This means that they can communicate, collaborate and co-ordinate in high performing teams without the need to be connected to the data-marts, OLAP databases and ERP systems which are the source of their management information.

ADBS supports the Habits of high-performing organizations in a single solution, including: a Balanced Scorecard and exception reporting for measurement; workflow support for action tracking; and an MI Catalog for cataloging of knowledge assets – all accessible according to the strategy and objectives to which they relate. The development of ADBS has been achieved by combining Arthur Andersen best practice with IBM/Lotus' Domino intranet and Notes technology.

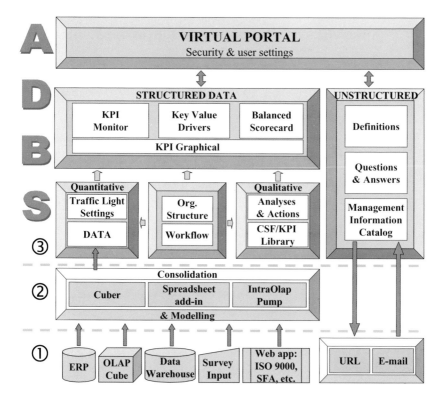

Figure E.1: Technical architecture of ADBS – see Key below

Key:
① = operational systems
② = middleware layer
③ = management information system

Functionality added to Lotus Notes and Domino by the Show Business toolset, which was used to create the ADBS system, includes:

- The Show Business toolset extends Notes and Domino allowing users to see charts and traffic light displays like the Balanced Scorecard of ADBS. These charts and tables of data are annotated with analysis and actions, which in turn are stored in Notes.

- The IntraOLAP database, which stores data in a Domino database in a way that it can be sliced and diced and drilled-down from a Notes or Web browser client. IntraOLAP data is said to be stored in 'Cubes'.

- Excel add-in which can create IntraOLAP cubes from within a spreadsheet.

- Cuber, which takes data from a Notes view and calculates KPIs, storing the result as Cubes of data in IntraOLAP format.

- IntraOLAP Pump, which takes data from OLAP databases and multi-dimensional report files and transfers it into Notes in IntraOLAP format.

To summarize, ADBS presents KPI information as Balanced Scorecards and action reports, etc. The KPI information is calculated by Cuber, from Notes Views, by an OLAP database and transferred into Notes by IntraOLAP Pump, or in a spreadsheet and transferred into Notes using a spreadsheet add-in.

Appendix F: Linking performance management with value-based management (VBM)

Today, organizations increasingly focus on long-term value creation in order to protect and maximize shareholder value. To measure the contribution to shareholder value, companies are increasingly implementing value-based management (VBM). This is much more than the selection of the key financial value drivers of the organization that measure value creation. It is the 'glue' that binds financial objectives, strategic plans and operational performance together into an integrated framework that involves all organizational levels.

At the corporate level, VBM concepts are used for portfolio management to identify those businesses, activities or projects to divest or in which to invest so as to improve value to stakeholders. At lower management levels, strategic plans are evaluated based on their ability to create value. When VBM is used at all management levels, the concepts of VBM are truly embedded in the organization. VBM concepts can be used to steer changes in behavior and to focus change management.

The challenge is to make VBM more than just the implementation of a new financial measure, to use it to relate strategy and operations at all levels of the organization.

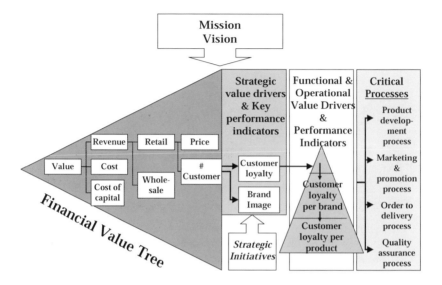

Figure F.1: The Financial Value Tree

VBM - The connection between strategic, financial and operational value drivers

The figure above shows how value creation can work in a practical way. The challenge is to keep the concept simple and easy to understand for everyone. Based on the vision and mission of the organization, the company is able to build a financial value tree. This value tree encompasses the key financial value drivers of the organization. The ultimate value driver in the financial value decomposition, such as Shareholder Value Added (SVA) or Economic Value Added (EVA^{TM}) [2] needs to be defined in a way that is easy to understand.

- [2] EVA is a trademark of Stern Stewart & Co.

Next, the strategic initiatives and plans are evaluated and prioritized according to their contribution to value creation. Grounded in these value-based initiatives, the organization is able to identify a limited set of key strategic value drivers and the performance indicators to measure them. For that reason the financial value tree is further extended to include non-financial value drivers also. These non-financial drivers are linked to the financial value drivers as much as possible. The causal relationships are often indirect or even systemic in nature (causal loops) and are difficult to calculate mathematically. The challenge for management is to quantify the relationship between leading non-financial and lagging financial value drivers, to have confidence in these links and at the same time to keep it simple.

The strategic value drivers and performance indicators are then translated into the lower organizational levels. In this case it is important to align the drivers and indicators with each other at all levels and with the respective strategic plans and initiatives at these levels.

Ultimately, VBM creates a link between financial value and the true drivers of value: business processes. The strategic, functional and operational value drivers and performance indicators (both financial and non-financial) measure the key value creation processes of the organization. By selecting the appropriate value drivers and performance indicators for each process, these processes can be measured on operational excellence and value creation.

A focus on value creation increases the overall performance and value creation ability of an organization since everyone in the organization, management as well as employees, sees and understands the link between their activities and their contribution to both the financial results and strategic objectives of the total organization. Also, value creation becomes measurable at every level of the organization giving it the focus and attention that it deserves from management at all levels.